Building Brand YOU!

A Step-by-Step Guide to Building Your Personal Brand

OMAR ABEDIN

Order this book online at www.trafford.com
or email orders@trafford.com

Most Trafford titles are also available at major online book retailers.

Print information available on the last page.

ISBN: 978-1-4907-6148-0 (sc)
ISBN: 978-1-4907-6149-7 (hc)
ISBN: 978-1-4907-6150-3 (e)

Library of Congress Control Number: 2015910160

Trafford rev.   06/30/2015

 www.trafford.com
North America & international
toll-free: 1 888 232 4444 (USA & Canada)
fax: 812 355 4082

Introduction
by Daniel Adams (my guru, mentor, & all-round great guy!)

If this book does nothing else it offers you a key you can use to open the door to the life and career meant for you.

The key is the idea that each of us needs to manage our brand identity. Just as products on the shelf need to be clear about the differences between them and their competitors, you and the others in the workplace are all seeking success and the pyramid gets narrower as we move up whatever ladder we are trying to climb. Developing a reputation is what we are working towards. But think about that for a moment. Having a reputation means having a reputation AS something.

Please note that in my first sentence, I said the career 'meant for you'. This may be quite different from the one you <u>think</u> you want.)

Each of us is endowed with talents, traits and values. Getting these aligned is all-important. You are who you are and others, believe it or not, actually sense the real you. Many years ago, I was mentored by John Crystal, the inspiration behind the famous book "What Color Is Your Parachute?"

John told us to remember: "What you are speaks so loudly I can hardly hear what you're saying."

After John's counsel, I changed careers and was able to put the real me to work wholeheartedly. I have been able to give all my energies to matters that interest me and feel important. Natural power seems to flow pretty effortlessly.

I have proven this principle in my own life and have made a career out of building powerful brand identities for companies and their brands and sub-brands.

I am honored to offer this small foreward. You are in wonderful hands. Omar Abedin impressed me from the first moment we met. Right away I saw him as a professional of very high intellectual ability coupled with a talent for simplifying complex ideas so they can be used. Omar loves to help and I feel sure if you work through this book, you'll find yourself possessing a valuable key.

Foreword

Over the past 20 years, I have had the privilege of working with some of the finest marketing brains, managing some of the finest brands for some of the finest companies in the world.

At the same time, with the arrival of social media technologies and smartphones, I've come to realize that in today's age, more so than perhaps at any point in our lives, WE have all become brands in our own rights.

Or perhaps I should say – we ALL have the opportunity to become brands. The reality, however, is that many of us, despite having an intense desire to be seen as "unique" & recognized as "different" by the world at large (witness the amount of User-Generated Content on YouTube!), and despite having hundreds of "friends" on FaceBook and LinkedIn, will never be more than commodities.

If that sounds harsh, I apologize. You see, a commodity is by definition something that can easily be replaced by another, similar, thing. On the other hand, a brand is irreplaceable. It is an integral part of our lives, and it is hard to examine just how important a role that brands play without thinking of myself – and indeed – all of US – as brands in our own right.

In my time managing brands, first as a corporate "brand" manager, and lately as a consultant who's raison d'être is helping people & companies "brand" better, I've learnt a few things and experimented with many tools... and I've been trying to figure out how those tools apply in our daily lives. The line between personal & professional domains continues to blur and the old nine-to-five mentality is practically non-existent. With the advent and huge popularity of smart phones, our online presence in now 24/7 – as is our availability to our employers, colleagues & clients. What does this mean for Brand "YOU"?

Well, as branding guru, and my friend & teacher, Daniel Adams says:

> "Every action you take
> is either a DEBIT from
> or a CREDIT to
> The Bank of Brand Equity."

Simply put – every thing you do either makes you MORE desirable – or LESS desirable – to your consumer & your shareholders.

What does "desirable" mean?

It means that as your value to your "consumer" (i.e. boss / employers / colleagues / clients) goes up – you are no longer seen as easily replaceable – and as a direct consequence – you are paid more, respected more, listened to more. Who among us does not wish to be valued more at work? After all, we spend the majority of our waking life either going to work, at work, or thinking about work.

It also means that your "shareholders" i.e. your family & loved ones – benefit more as a result of the higher value attached to you, the strongly-branded employee.

And for YOU? Well, it gives you a game plan that works. You will be able to take control of your fate, developing a powerful perception plan that differentiates you from the masses – and your competition. And you will learn how to bring that to life – and make real changes in your life to BE that more valuable, differentiated, BRANDED person – with all the positives & concrete benefits that accrue to you as a result.

The purpose of this book is to lay these ideas out for you in a simple and direct manner, avoiding as far as possible the complexity that sometimes makes the subject of branding so confusing to the "non-marketing" folks among us.

If you are a marketing professional, these ideas will resonate with you immediately, and at a gut level. If you are not, don't worry - it may take a little bit of discipline and rigour upfront, but a great deal of reward WILL follow, provided you follow the guidelines in spirit (if not in word ☺).

So what does that mean? Well, for starters, it means that I'm going to try to keep the jargon to a minimum. I can't do away with it altogether – and you need to know some of the "marketing speak" - but I will do my best to ensure that it does not get in the way of your learning.

What else? It means that this book draws on the collective knowledge of many people - especially Dan Adams. Dan is the CEO of the Daniel Adams Co. in the US, and an incredibly knowledgeable & insightful marketing genius. He has forgotten more about Brand Equity than most of us will ever know. Dan and I first met in the early nineties, when he had come to train the marketing team of the company that I worked with at the time. It was an unforgettable experience, and one that stayed with me for over fifteen years, when we met again. His impact in my life, and his contribution to the world of branding - has been nothing short of astronomical.

At seventy, Dan remains a force of nature. He is my guru, and my mentor, and many of the concepts that I will discuss here either originate with him, or have been clarified for me by Dan. You see dear Reader, where Dan's true genius comes to the fore is the ability to take complex ideas and break them down to the simplest common denominator, so that they become instantly clear and self-evident truths to even the rankest of beginners in the field.

So here we go. Hopefully, this book will cast some light on what many consider to be the (black) art & science that is branding & marketing – and it's practical application to building your personal brand. I believe it's a little of both, and done well, it is nothing short of magic.

Happy reading.

Omar Abedin

Table of Contents

CHAPTER 1

What is a Brand anyway? (...And why YOU should want to be one!)?

Brands are ubiquitous. There is hardly a category in our overly complicated lives where brands do not play an important role – one far more important than we are perhaps willing or able to admit. We adore them. We associate ourselves with their icons. We flash them to friends and complete strangers. We carry them in our hands, around our necks, over our shoulders. We drive around in them. We give them to our friends and family. We immerse ourselves in them in so many ways that sometimes we would be hard pushed to name them, or count them.

So, if you agree that brands are everywhere, how do we define exactly what a brand is? This is at once easier and harder than it sounds... After all, we all know a brand when we see one. Whether it is a phone, laptop, purse, suit, watch, or car, we know what we like. In that sense, it's a bit like art. We can all say whether something appeals to us, but it is far more difficult to say exactly why. Therein lies the challenge. So before we move ahead, lets agree on a working definition.

I've heard literally dozens of definitions, each one better than the last. There are extremely complicated ones, and extremely simple ones. The one I like best, developed by Dan Adams of the Daniel Adams Co, goes something like this:

"A brand is a set of ideas and associations that exists in the mind.

A product or service exists only when we see it, or use it...

If hearing the name, or seeing it's symbol triggers a set of associations, it is a brand.

Otherwise – it's just a product."

What are the critical pieces of this definition?

Lets start with ideas and associations. Whenever you think of a brand, there are certain associations that immediately come to mind. Lets take an example of McDonalds to illustrate the point. If we were to ask a consumer of McDonalds what they associated with the brand, this is what they would probably say:

American style fast food (Mc everything)
The yellow 'M'
Kids play area
Same menu everywhere
Ronald McDonald
Cheerful service
Clean restrooms

The amazing thing is that whether you ask people in the US, England, Brazil, Russia, China, Pakistan or Australia – they will say EXACTLY the same thing. Really. We call this the Brand Fire Dance, and it is one of the key characteristics of a powerful brand. In fact, the greater the number of associations, and the more clear they are to the consumer, the more powerful the brand.

Each of these associations also triggers the others. When you see the yellow 'M', you suddenly have an image of golden fries, a Big Mac, and a huge Coke. Your stomach starts growling too. ☺

Another characteristic of a power brand is that it has a zone of authority within which it operates. It is seen as the expert in that domain. E.g. Apple owns coolness in the technology arena. Even if you are not a fan of Apple, you will be hard pushed not to acknowledge the oomph value of any of their offerings.

Lastly, we have a strong personal connection with the brands in our lives. We – dare I say it – love them. Sometimes, we commit murder to possess them (remember the runner killed in Central Park for their Nikes?). How many of us will admit that our personal identity – our self-image – is closely tied into, and driven by the brands we use?

So, if you were asked to list your top 10 brands today, this might be a more difficult task than might appear on its face. After all, there are so many... how to choose? What makes it even more challenging is that sometimes, celebrities are promoting the brands we choose. These celebs are brands in their own right, a fact that the brands that hire them are fully aware of, and in fact, counting on to build awareness of their brands. These celebs exude such star power that we all – almost without exception – know them.

Brands like Barack Obama... Oprah Winfrey... Bruce Springsteen... Hannah Montana... Adolf Hitler... Tony Blair... Abraham Lincoln... Winston Churchill... Nixon... Michael Jackson... Princess Diana... Elvis Presley... Mohammed Ali (Cassius Clay)...

The list is huge even without religious figures (!)... However, with each and every one of these strongly branded individuals, we are instantly taken to a different place. We feel we knew them, what they were striving for, indeed the very value system that they represented and fought for. We don't have to like it, but we know it.

Why do we remember these people? Why do millions continue to worship at the altar of some, and continue to question the motives of others years, decades and even centuries after they are dead?

The answer is simple – we know what they stood for. We knew exactly what their stance was in life. What they valued. Where they came from. We loved the little quirks in their personalities. We embraced what they embodied... and the truly amazing thing is – they embody those things today.

How can this be? How can someone who died hundreds (thousands?) of years ago continue to own a slice of our conscious (and unconscious) minds?

So, my question to you right now is: What do YOU stand for?

Is there something you do, some belief you hold, some personality trait – anything – that makes you – YOU?

I want you to think about that for 5 minutes, and if you are not able to identify anything of value immediately, DON'T panic. Read on, and by the time we are done, you should be in a very different place. If on the other hand, you are able to identify multiple things, then you have probably gone too broad, and what you have identified is not unique, differentiated or ownable enough to create value for you.

While you are thinking of this, you will come to understand a little bit of the dilemma faced by marketers & brand builders every day. The need to make your brand stand out is paramount in the minds of such people – it burns hot in their minds and hearts. For a brand to be seen as undifferentiated usually means death in the near term.

For people, it's not much different. If you fail to maximize your "brand equity", it usually means that you will end up in a dead-end job, with an unsatisfactory personal life, always wondering why you are on the outside looking in. Your earnings potential will remain unrealized.

The bad news is – this is the case for the vast majority of working people today.

The good news is – there is a way to fix this situation, and it starts right here & now.

CHAPTER 2

Why is it so difficult to build a Brand (specially your OWN!)?

Given the pervasiveness of brands & branding in our lives, why is it so difficult to create a powerful brand? BTW, in case you were wondering... the number of brands that you are aware of as a consumer is a TINY fraction of the total number of brands that are out there. That includes all those brands that are launched every year, most with some level of fanfare, only to fail in the market.

Think about it. There are literally thousands of beverage brands around the world, but you would be hard pushed to name 1% of them (unless of course you work in the industry.) ☺

So, why is building a brand so challenging, even for companies that depend on brands for their very existence?

Well, for starters, **the brand-building role is seldom stated** (there are of course many exceptions to this at a corporate level. Proctor & Gamble, Unilever, Nestle and many more do this very well!) However, when we apply this to building our own personal brands, it becomes the rule rather than the exception.

Certainly, people like Richard Branson of Virgin have set about building their personal brands with clear & compelling objectives. But the majority of us do not see ourselves as brands. We don't explicitly state this even to ourselves, and because we don't, we are hardly likely to achieve brand status in our lifetimes.

However – once you start seeing yourself as a BRAND – and start working on all that comes with it, your world changes completely. You may be cynical now, & I can almost see you shaking your head... but read on, and we will talk again later. ☺

Secondly, **brand equity is intangible**. For most people – even those deeply immersed in the practice of marketing – defining brand equity can be a challenge. And if you can't define it, then how on earth can you possibly quantify it? Well, I'm here to tell you that not only is it possible to measure brand equity without an advanced degree in marketing, it is imperative that brands measure their equity on an on-going basis.

The fact is that there are companies dedicated to carrying out this very exercise for large and well-known brands. In some cases, they have been known to carry out this exercise for High Net Worth Individuals (the very, very wealthy!). But is it possible for you to measure your own brand equity?

Yes. It takes a little bit of common sense figuring out, but it can be done, and once you have learnt the process, it's quite easy to repeat. And you should repeat it quite regularly. In fact, I would suggest that you add a brand equity index to your New Year's resolutions – because once you start measuring it, you will want to track it to see how you are doing!

Thirdly, **there are always short-term pressures**. We face decisions daily, hourly, that determine how our brand equity is going to move. In fact, every decision we make, every action we take, leads to either a deposit into the Bank of Brand Equity, or a withdrawal from there. If you start thinking of it in those terms, you will start to see the impact – positive or negative – on your Brand Equity balance.

Confused? Don't be. Let's take an example. Jane is an accountant. She makes $150 K a year, has great perks, a nice office and a company car. There's only one problem. She HATES her job. She hates her boss, her work, her commute... she is deeply unhappy. This unhappiness translates into a stressed relationship with her spouse, and a non-existent one with her teenage daughter. And yet, she continues at her job, day in and day out, because that's all she knows. Her confusion & anger grows, until one day her long-suffering husband moves out, and her daughter moves away to college. Unable to cope with the changes in her environment, and unable to understand how these have come about, Jane enters into a long-term therapy program. Eventually she comes to terms with her "issues"... or most of them.

Now what if Jane had laid out her Brand Identity early on? Perhaps things might have been different.

In fact, once you have gone through the exercise yourself, you will come to realize that it would almost certainly have led her down a different path. And whichever path she had eventually chosen, she would have led a more fulfilling life overall – one with less of the negativity and stress of living a life that just is not YOU.

The fourth obstacle to building brands that confronts many companies is what I call **"revolving brand managers"**. Young, energetic people, some straight out of school, are assigned the responsibility of managing a brand, or brands. Many of these people – these brand managers – have only one objective: to build as many bullet points on their CV as possible in as short a time as possible, in order to maximize their growth trajectory, either in their current company or in another company. This is not necessarily a bad thing, and these are by no means bad people. It's just that in their hurry to add talking points to their CVs, they sometimes do things that are not in the best interests of the brand that has been entrusted to their care. For example, a brand built on the quality of its offering might find itself a "football" in a price war amongst different retailers just so that a short-term gain in market share can be reported in the monthly report that goes to management. It does not seem to matter that the equity – the value – of the brand has been diminished in the eyes of its consumers. All that matters is that the market share blip was duly reported to management, and the brand manager's "performance" recognized, either through a bonus, a promotion, or both.

Well, you might say that as the brand manager for your OWN brand, you don't have that problem, and on the face of it, you would be right. After all, you are in control of your own destiny, right?

Right?

Perhaps not all the time... How many people do you know who seem intent on shooting themselves in the foot ALL the time? Self-inflicted injuries are more common than perhaps we realize.

You may have heard the parable of the elephant and the chain? When the elephant was a child, it was chained to a concrete pillar by the leg. Whenever it had the urge to seek freedom it found that it was unable to move, and over time, the chain became the reality. After that, and even when the chain was long gone, the elephant remained by the pillar because it was the only reality that it knew.

Therapy and analysis can help us understand just how much of the situation we are in is self-inflicted... or in our own minds. How many of us are stuck in dead end jobs, but inexplicably refuse to move to another role? How many people do you know who recognize that their current qualifications, degrees, certifications etc. are not what the market needs, but are unable to make the decision to GET new degrees? Of course there are short-term pressures – we talked about that already. Who among us is free of those pressures?

What separates the truly successful and happy people among us from the rest is the recognition that how they spend their time upon this earth should be a reflection of who they wish to be, or in some cases, to become. So we read about the billionaires who give away their entire wealth to serve humanity. And we see teachers, policemen, firefighters, nurses and many others around us, serving the community in their own way, happy & content in the knowledge that they are making a difference in people's lives.

The key lies in knowing who you are as a person – identifying a clear & compelling Brand Identity for yourself that states EXACTLY who you are, or wish to be. It should be as clear & powerful as you can make it, and hopefully, it will resonate with you in such a way that only you could possibly bring it to life. More on that later.

The fifth and final obstacle to building a brand – and our OWN brand – is that **we seldom take the time to truly measure brand equity**. The major reason for this is that, even if we recognize the importance of measuring our equity, it seems an impossible task. After all, equity is intangible, right?

Not so. Anything can be measured, and if we take a bit of time to define what it is that we wish to measure, we can certainly come up with ways and means to measure our growth or improvements in those areas. There are more details in Chapter 8, the section on score-carding, so don't worry about it. You will get there soon enough.

CHAPTER 3

What is Brand Equity? (And do you know what you stand for in the mind of your key consumer?)

There are hundreds of definitions for this concept, from the very sophisticated and theoretical, to the downright earthy and practical. I tend to lean towards this latter end of the spectrum, because as my guru Dan Adams likes to prove time and again – true genius lies in the ability to take complex concepts & ideas and break them down to a level of simplicity that anyone with an IQ over 70 can easily understand. So here is my preferred definition of this concept.

A brand's equity is... everything that must travel with it if it moves to a new company.

Sounds simple? Let's look at a couple of examples. When the Procter & Gamble Company acquired the Gillette brand of shaving products for men a few years ago, it paid north of $20 billion dollars for that brand, and what it stood for in the minds of consumers around the world.

Wrap your head around that for a second please. P&G did not pay this sizeable amount for the factories, the offices, the investments and other physical assets of the Gillette Company, although they were no doubt included in the terms of the sale. No, what got the Board of P&G so excited was the chance to own one of the strongest brands in the personal care category – and what it stood for in the minds of consumers. Gillette stands for "The Best a Man Can Get" in any language in any country in the world. Now that is equity.

So- what do YOU stand for? Do you know? Can you even say it to yourself, let alone communicate it to others?

Let's take another example. The Disney Company recently paid almost $30 billion for the Marvel Company (you know them as the people behind the Incredible Hulk, Spiderman, X-Men etc.). What did the Board of Disney – which by the way stands for the hard-nosed idea of "The Magical Family Experience" – see in a bunch of super hero brands? Because, let's face it, they paid $30 billion for a bunch of cartoon characters.

This acquisition was a great idea for a number of reasons, but what is amazing is that there were no "assets" etc. of any significance involved in the deal. The bulk of the deal was based on quantifying the intangible value of the Marvel brands – and that is what brand equity is all about really.

So coming back to the earlier question – what does YOUR brand stand for? Start thinking now please, as you read on.

In both the above examples, companies were willing to pay huge amounts of money for intangible things. Why? Well, there are many reasons – strategic fit, new consumer base – and so on. More importantly, how is this relevant to you? Well, the skills, competencies, attitudes and approaches that YOU bring to the table are unique to you – and totally intangible. How you bring them to life for your consumer – your employer – and how they perceive the value of those intangibles, will define how you are "valued". Quite literally...

Look around at your colleagues, the men and women with whom you are spending the day. Is everyone at the same pay scale? Is everyone receiving the same perks? Does everyone have a corner office?

The answer is obviously – no. But why is this? Yes, of course there are rational reasons. Education is one of them. Experience is another. But more often than not, it is the intangible reasons that differentiate the average office worker from the star. Think about it.

Can you quantify a positive attitude? A welcoming smile? A can-do attitude? But think about co-workers who are grouchy, grumpy and unwelcoming – do you feel like asking them for anything? What about the sloppy, poorly-groomed and worse-dressed co-worker who doesn't bother with small niceties such as deodorant, pressed clothes or exploring the fringe benefits of owning a razor? Do you like spending time with them? Or do you talk with them quickly and make an excuse to move on before they can even start to dazzle you with their brilliance and erudition?

On the other hand, we all know someone that we love to talk to, for any number of reasons. They are warm and welcoming, and even if they are exceptionally busy, they will take out a moment where we have their undivided attention.

So – coming back to the original question. **What is your brand equity?** It is all those things that go with you if you leave your current job and move to a new role or a new company. Usually this means just YOU – and the clothes on your back. While the clothes you wear are important, as are your personal habits and other "physical" things that people can see, far more important – and indeed usually the reason you got the new role in the first place – is what you carry around inside your head.

What you know is of course critical... if you are not qualified to have your job, the chances that you will get it, or keep it for long, are fairly remote. But if you are competing for a plum role against another candidate with similar educational background and work experience as yourself, guess what make one of you more attractive to your potential employer.

That's right, your attitudes, your beliefs, your value system... in short, everything that makes you – YOU.

The question really is – what are your attitudes, beliefs, values etc? And how do these key elements actually differentiate you from anyone else, and make you valuable to your employer – current & potential? How does this maximize your Brand Equity?

If you can't answer these questions, neither can anyone else ☺

Read on please.

CHAPTER 4

Which are you – Product or Brand?
(How do you know?)

Let us agree at the outset that a Brand is not the same as a Product. I think you know this already at a gut level, because we all know people who go out and spend hundreds if not thousands of dollars on a bag that carries the LV brand. I mean, really? It's just a bag, right? Wrong!

If you think that "it's just a bag", you probably believe that everyone who buys one of those "bags" must be totally nuts. Well, assuming that a fair proportion of those people have way too much money and time on their hands, but are not actually certifiable, why do they invest in these "bags"?

It's because **that brand has come to mean something that transcends** the mere physical characteristics of a "bag". In fact, referring to an LV as just a "bag" is enough to have you ostracized in certain circles ☺

Let's look at another example. Let's say that I offer you a choice between two watches. Watch 'A' tells the time with an analog display, shows you the date, has glow in the dark numbers, is water-resistant to a hundred meters, and has an extra hand for the 12/24 mark. Watch 'B' has all that and more. It has a modern digital display that allows you to flip between the 12 and 24-hour format at the touch of a button. It has a nightlight, and special features for nighttime usage. It also has a timer, three alarms with daily, weekday & weekend options, a chronograph with lap option, a 100-hour countdown timer, and a second time zone with date!

Which watch do you prefer?

It doesn't really matter which you choose –
Watch 'A' or 'B'

But what if I reveal to you that watch 'A' is a Rolex worth $5000, and watch 'B' is a Timex worth $50. Does it change the way you feel about the two watches? I'm pretty sure it does.

Why is this? Let's try to define the difference between a brand and a product. At what point does a product cease to be a product, and transition to a brand? I think most of us have some sort of idea, and probably could get to it at some point. Here is a solid working definition that might help to clear up the difference between a product and a brand in your mind.

A product is a thing on a shelf...

A brand is an idea in the mind.

A product is in our minds only when we see it, or use it. But a brand exists in our minds as a set of ideas and associations.

If hearing the name or seeing the symbol triggers stored images in your mind, it's a brand – if not, it is just a product!

OK, let's do a quick exercise. We'll call it a "quick take" on two well-known and respected brands – McDonalds & Burger King. Taking just 5 minutes for each brand, I want you to write down in as much detail as possible what you know about the following:

	McDonalds	Burger King
Product Offerings (What does it sell?)		
Characteristic Attributes (What you can always expect it to be!)		
Symbols & Signals (Logos, Colours, Slogans)		
Brand Personality (Brand as a Person)		
History & Reputation (Brand Folklore)		

Associated Benefits (Functional, Emotional and/or Sensorial)		
Core Consumers (Who loves it the most?)		
Market Position / Role (Pioneer, Leader, Follower)		
Brand Capsule (Consumer's Core Idea of it)		

Having completed this exercise, I'd like you to go ahead and rate the relative strength of these brands on a scale of 1 to 10. How rich, relevant and consistent do you find these brands to be?

Let me play the role of prognosticator for a second and say that you rated McDonalds higher than BK. Did you? Well, you are not alone. In fact, having run this exercise in many corners of the globe, I can tell you that Mickey Dees as it is affectionately known, gets a higher score from Kuala Lumpur to Karachi, from New York to Nairobi.

Why? Well, it's complicated and really simple at the same time. To break it down, McDonalds does certain things really well, and does them consistently, in every location in every market that it operates in (which is pretty much the entire world at this point). I'm going to list them for you here, but if I gave you two minutes, I bet you would come up with the exact same list (give or take one or two items). Here is what makes McDonalds "McDonalds":

1. The golden arches
2. The play area
3. The clown
4. The food (love it or hate it, it tastes exactly the same everywhere!)
5. The restrooms
6. Add your own item here _____

This "fire-dance" of associations is really what it all boils down to. A power brand has many such associations. They are strong & clearly defined, and they connect with and support each other. All together, they are synergistic, and their value grows exponentially. 1+1+1 = 5.

SO... **If I ask you to list down the attributes that are associated with you, what will they be?** More importantly, if I ask your key customers – your family, friends, colleagues, superiors & others who interact with you regularly – will they list the same attributes, in the same order of importance? If you imagine that those lists will be the same as your list, you have another thing coming. Seriously. I'm not kidding.

As an example, if you think that your sense of humour is one of your defining traits, your "customers" will see it in ways as far removed from one another as "he's irritating the way he constantly has to joke around" to "clown" to "what a &*^%!" to simply "Oh my God here he comes again, where can I hide?"... I'm not saying that a few people won't "get" you on this attribute – they well might. But the spread of the perception will quite literally shock you.

Try this – if you dare. Ask your "customers" for feedback on your defining attributes. But be warned – you may not like the answers you receive. Handling tough feedback is never easy – it can feel like a wet fish in the face. The first thing you do after you receive critical feedback is – take a deep breath. Say thank you because you KNOW that feedback of any kind – if honestly given – is a GIFT of monumental proportions. Accept it with gratitude, before you rip it open and try to digest its contents. Take your time over this. Internalize it before you reject it out of hand – we all know that tendency. Don't give in to it. After this, take another deep breath and start analyzing the details. You will be fine – trust me. But it is an uncomfortable process, even at the best of times. And at the worst? Well, it can change your life, but not in the way that you expect.

If the feedback that you get is clear, consistent and shows a link to the person who provided the feedback, you are a brand to that person, or on the way to becoming one. If not, then you need to bring some focus to this area of your life. Remember, at this point we are not "judging" the brand values – only whether you are actually a brand or not.

So, what do you think? **Are you a brand in your own right?** Let's find out.

CHAPTER 5

Building Power Brands (it's not a black art once you know how!)

A power brand has certain characteristics.

Each power brand has an owned zone of authority.

1. It has distinctive associations that are unique to that brand.
2. Each association triggers the other, and the brand.
3. It has a powerful personal bond with its core consumer.

Let's look at some examples. What brand is this?
- Created for top athletes
- On the sidelines of major games
- It's all about SWEAT
- Lightning bolt
- Poured over the coach's head by the winner

The chances are that if you fit a certain demographic & psychographic profile you guessed that this is Gatorade® even if that brand is not available where you happen to live.

How about this one?

- User-friendly technology
- Computer for "creatives"
- Digital innovator
- Digital music leader
- Stylishly cool

Again, whether you are an Apple® fan or not, you probably guessed which brand this refers to.

Let's look at ourselves. Can you identify certain attributes that fit the bill here? Is there something that you are good at – I mean really, really, good at? For example, do you know cars better than anyone you know? Can you argue longer and harder than anyone you know? These are zones of authority that you can own – they are neither good nor bad – but they can be owned if they support your overall attempts at building a power brand identity for yourself.

What about associations? **What do people think of when they think of you?** Snappy dresser? A ladies' man? Studious nerd? Brilliant conversationalist? Try to list the top five things that you think describe you best – and see whether people – your customers – have a similar view. Be prepared to be surprised.

Do your associations trigger each other? For example – if you are a talker, are you also seen as a great friend? Or a great conversationalist? Or a great lawyer? You see how this works...

And last, **do your "customers" feel strongly about you as a brand?** Positive or negative is not the question at this point – it's the strength of the connection that we are interested in right now. People could hate you – that would still make you a brand, although most of us prefer not to be that type of brand.

No, its only when people are indifferent towards you that you should be concerned – but not for long. With the tools you are picking up right here, that won't be a problem for long!

Now, in case you are wondering how this exercise is done for humans ☺ as opposed to fast-moving consumer products, let's take a look at a couple of examples. See if you can guess who these people are.

- Larger-than-life leader
- Insists on having fun at work
- Known for crazy stunts (this should be enough to guess who we are talking about ☺
- Passionate about delighting customers
- Believes in innovation at all cost

Yes, you guessed it, its Richard Branson, who is arguably as big a brand as his famous Virgin brand.

How about this person?

- Idiosyncratic silicon valley guy
- Designs the coolest gadgets ever
- Launched the first range of commercial home computers
- Passionate about delighting customers
- Believes in innovation at all cost

You had him at "coolest gadgets", right? Mr. Steve Jobs is such a huge brand that personal news about him – good or bad - could move Apple share prices up and down like a yoyo. RIP Steve.

This exercise can – and must – be carefully thought-through and consistently executed in order for it to make sense, but it can be done for every major and minor celebrity the world has ever seen. In fact, the ease with which we complete this exercise for a person is directly proportional to the quantum of their celebrity.

So, now that we know what qualities or attributes a power brand must possess, how do we actually go about building a power brand?

It is as simple as follows:

- **STEP 1: Insight development** – Understand what your key customers really want or need. Are you currently fulfilling that need? Can it be done better? Could the people you love – and you - be happier? Is it worth it? You tell me.

- **STEP 2: Design the product** – Since that's you, this requires looking at all aspects of who you are, pulling it apart, and putting it back together again. The re-building process is a tough one, requires a lot of time investment, feedback from those who care, and constant tweaking and evaluation as things progress.

- **STEP 3: Develop a Brand Identity** – a plan for how you wish to be perceived. This is a rigorous exercise that demands time and attention, while staying grounded in reality. For example, for the majority of us, striving to look like Brad Pitt or Angelina Jolie on any given day is challenging to say the least. But that doesn't mean that we shouldn't try to spruce ourselves up as much as we can to reflect the brand that we wish to become. The opposite might apply for a rock band member, who has completely different criteria, and a different frame of reference within which he / she is operating. So this is a critical piece of the process.

- **STEP 4: Develop a Marketing Mix** – how you are going to bring your Brand Identity to life. You might develop a truly unique Brand Identity that you can own, but if you don't make the effort to bring it to life, it won't be worth the paper it's written on.

- **STEP 5: Time and consistency** – you need to give yourself time. You cannot change into someone else, or even change anything significant about yourself – I mean really change – overnight. It's not possible, or even desirable. You need to put together a structure and act on it. For example, trying to lose 50 pounds in a month is guaranteed to fail, even if you possess the willpower of a Gandhi. Once you stop fasting and working out like a crazy person, you will inevitably put the weight back on. Instead, putting together a well-thought-out diet plan with a simple exercise plan allows you to take off between 1-2 pounds a week for 25 weeks, and is a strategy that is far more likely to succeed, with long-term ramifications. It is easier to preach it than to practice it though, because people are generally aware of how to change their body shapes to get closer to their self-image. However, the rate of obesity in the general population is ballooning out of control. So, action – specific, focused, action over time is critical.

All of this sounds easy, right? RIIIIIGHT! So now you know that there is a five-step process to achieving Brand status, what's holding you back? Only YOU!

CHAPTER 6

The Brand Equity cause-and-effect model (are you focusing on the right things?)

Let's recap our definition of Brand Equity from Chapter 3.

A brand's equity is... everything that must travel with it if it moves to a new company. In your case, if you move to another company, role or assignment, what are the things that move with you? Mostly intangible things, you say... things that are hard to measure or define? Hmm. You could be right, but on the other hand...

Let's take a look at possibly one of the most important cause & effect ladders you will ever see.

1. **Every company and brand that I have ever worked with has wanted more sales.** "Higher Revenue!" has been the rallying cry at all of sales and marketing conferences that I have attended over the years. It's also been the mantra for almost every senior executive that I have spoken with in that time. This, and how to achieve the continuous growth in the topline, has been the driver behind many a corporate program, restructuring,

or executive realignment. In our case, we are talking about your compensation. Your salary package... the amount of money that your company pays you for the services that you provide them. That is a reflection of the "value" society in general, and your company (and boss) in particular, attach to you.

2. **But what drives revenue?** Revenue in the consumer products world is a function of how many cases you can ship from a factory. But in your case, it is a function of your output – its volume, and its value. How much you produce is definitely going to impact how much someone values you. A person churning out the work of 3 will be valued (ideally) far more than the average employee. But its not just about how much you churn out, since the average person works a heck of a lot of hours. No, it is more about the quality of what you do... and whatever else you that makes you unique. Do you write? Do you blog? Are you a recognized authority in your field? Are you the go-to person within your department for your area of expertise? So, how do you go about improving the "perceived quality" of your work?

3. **Understanding what constitutes "value" to your key stakeholders is the key.** If you can understand that well, you can take informed decisions that better position you against those key needs. For example, if you know that your boss is under tremendous pressure

to deliver a project against tight deadlines, and you can support that effort through working long hours & weekends without being asked, and with a positive attitude, then you are the man. However, if you decide to call in sick on Monday after partying too hard on the weekend, then probably not…

4. So, now that you know what constitutes value, **understand what perceptions you need to create in the minds of your key constituents** to be seen as the champion of value at home, at work and in your social circle. Once you nail those perceptions, it is a relatively straightforward task to start managing those perceptions.

So… in reality, if you want to maximize your "revenue" – **your main job is creating & managing perceptions.**

The first time I came to this realization, it blew my mind.

Have you thought about yourself in this light? That while you might be a business development manager, a pharmacist, a fireman or a news anchor, your real job – if you want to maximize your life – is to create and manage expectations and perceptions. Wow.

So how do you do this? Here's how…

CHAPTER 7

The Road to building YOUR brand equity (definitely the road less travelled)

Step 1: Spend some time understanding the real needs of your "customers" – your family, friends and employer.

In the business world, this is called "consumer insight development". Find out what is important to the people who matter in your life, how they feel about you and your role, what really makes them tick... Once you know what counts, you can start positioning yourself to maximize the way your efforts are recognized. The important thing to remember here is that "Perception is Reality". At work, if you are not able to make your contributions transparent to your boss, your co-workers and the management, the chances are that your efforts will be minimally recognized, and you will find yourself with feelings of bitterness and anxiety. Now, please understand – I am not for one minute advocating that you try to create a perception that is not founded in reality, or try to take credit for the work of others. That puts you squarely in the "pointy-haired boss" category and you will rightly become the target of your co-workers' wrath. No. I'm saying do the work, and do it in such a way that it could only have come from you. The same applies at home, and in your social circle.

But how do you leverage the insights you develop to maximize your "value" and the "revenue" that flows from it?

Step 2: Develop your Brand Identity (Brand ID). We will talk at length about this later, but it involves developing a signature style for the way you do things – an unmistakable stamp that tells the world that this is something only you could have created, only you could have worked on and delivered. Its like a watermark on a document – it always shows up, even in photocopies, and it is easily recognizable as yours.

In order to build a powerful Brand ID, you need to know what you stand for currently – what your Brand ID is today- and what you are going to stand for in the future – in the minds, hearts & wallets of the people who matter in your life... your family, your friends, and your employer.

So, how do you find out what you stand for now? It's easy – just ask. Be prepared for the answers to be very different to what you have in your mind, though. As brand managers are often shocked at how consumers actually perceive the brands that they manage when they get the results of research, you will almost certainly be surprised at how people perceive you, and how they attach value to the things that you do, your behaviour, personality and so much more... But ask, and say thank you for the feedback you receive.

Step 3: Bring your desired brand identity to life. How do you go about bringing your desired perceptions alive in the minds of the people who matter? What do you have to do to be seen the way you really want to be seen? Again, let me stress that I'm not talking about smoke-and-mirrors. People see through that sooner rather than later. No, you have to take action – but in a planned, concerted effort that maximizes the perception value of what you are doing. It helps to think of this is a bank account, with deposits that build your perception and equity, and withdrawals that don't.

Remember, in the words of the inimitable Dan Adams – "every step or action you take will either be a deposit into, or a withdrawal from, the bank of your brand equity."

So – be careful. You can spend years building the balance in your brand equity bank, and blow it all because of one stupid thing that leaves you high and dry – and deep in the red.

Step 4: Invest. Your time, energy, and focus needs to be dedicated to building the desired Brand ID in the minds and hearts of your constituents. And it will take time, energy and focus. Think of any iconic brand, and you will find a history and a heritage of actions taken by that brand that have gone into building the perception that you have in your mind today... it's the same with people. Richard Branson has a well-known penchant for a certain type of activity – and all his "stunts" are cleverly designed to build his personal and business brand equities in a particular direction. Love him or hate him, you certainly can't ignore him.

Step 5: Close the loop. Talk to your "consumers" on a regular basis. See how your perceptions are varying, changing... and they will change. Monitor them, and you will know whether you are on track to achieve your goals. They will appreciate the effort you are making to improve, and they will help you. Those who won't provide you with feedback probably wouldn't help you anyway, so don't worry about them. Do what needs to be done, and move on. Be all that you can be – start today.

CHAPTER 8

Measuring Brand Equity (measure progress or forget it!)

measuring up

Brands spend a lot of time measuring the key drivers of their equity (or they should be!). They have teams monitoring how they are doing in the market, and how consumers are thinking, feeling and talking about them. Now, you don't have a team that can help you track your brand equity, right? Wrong.

Your team is comprised of those people who are important to you, and those who care about you. Possible "Team You" membership could comprise your boss, your mentor (if you don't have one, get one!), some close co-workers, your wife (or significant other), and some of your close friends and confidantes.

Set-up a process – formal at work, and informal at home and with friends – to gather the feedback that you NEED to know whether you are moving in the right direction or not. Once the process is set up, you need to decide what you are going to track. This really depends on what your brand is going to stand for, but here are some examples of possible things to measure or track on an on-going basis, and the people to ask the questions to:

BOSS: On a scale of 1 to 10 (10 being the highest), how much do you, my BOSS, agree with the following:

1. I'm your go-to person for issues in my area.
2. I'm trustworthy.
3. I'm aligned to your goals, and do everything in my power to help you achieve those goals.
4. I'm an expert in my area.
5. I'm the most valuable member in your team.
6. I work well with others.
7. I demonstrate & embody the values that you expect of members in your team.
8. I'm likeable, and I make an effort to get along with co-workers and colleagues.
9. I'm networked internally and externally.
10. I'm well regarded by senior management (your constituents).

CO-WORKERS: On a scale of 1 to 10 (10 being the highest), how much do you, my CO-WORKER, agree with the following:

1. I'm your go-to person for issues in my area.
2. I'm trustworthy.
3. I'm aligned to your goals, and do everything in my power to help you achieve those goals.
4. I'm an expert in my area.
5. My inputs are valuable to you in your daily work.
6. I work well with others.
7. I demonstrate & embody the values that you expect of members in our team.

8. I'm likeable, and I make an effort to get along with co-workers and colleagues.
9. I'm networked internally and externally.
10. I'm well regarded by senior management (our constituents).

SPOUSE / SIGNIFICANT OTHER: On a scale of 1 to 10 (10 being the highest), how much do you, my SPOUSE, agree with the following:

1. I'm there for you when you need me.
2. I'm trustworthy.
3. I'm aligned to your goals, and do everything in my power to help you achieve those goals.
4. I'm an expert in my area, and I use my expertise to make our lives better.
5. My inputs are valuable to you in your daily life.
6. I show you how much I care on a regular basis.
7. I demonstrate & embody the values that you expect, and that we agree on.
8. I'm likeable, and I make an effort to get along with our family and friends.
9. I love you.
10. We are in it for the long haul – I see us together till death do us part (not in a creepy way ☺).

Once you get the results, put them on a spreadsheet and really understand what they mean to you. Again, the statements above will vary from person to person, and will hold different levels of importance for different people. You might have only 5 really important ones and that's fine. The key thing is to not stop this process, since the initial reading is just that – a start point. It's where you are today, or where you are seen to be, which is the same thing. What matters is the NEXT reading, and the one after that – have you managed to move the needle on the things that matter to you? And in what direction?

If nothing has changed, don't worry about it. Moving the needle on important things takes time, and maybe enough time has not passed yet for your behaviour changes or new actions to be noticed. Don't sweat it. Keep on doing it.

If on the other hand, scores on some key parameters have moved downwards, then probe to find out why in a non-confrontational way. You need to understand what is not working, and why, so that you can fix it. Once you do fix it, put your head down and make it true. You & only you can do it. And you must.

Make this a life-long discipline, and once you have it down, and your scores on your key metrics are moving upwards nicely, you can reduce the frequency of the feedback. But don't stop it because you then run the risk of backsliding and losing all the gains that you have made in your development. And that would just be a shame.

CHAPTER 9

Doing a Quick Take on YOU (much harder than it sounds)

Remember the quick take you did on the burger brands in Chapter 4? Now, you need to do the same exercise for yourself. A quick review of who you are... through the eyes of a marketer. Remember, you are the Chief Marketing Officer of Brand YOU. Here is the form – please keep your responses simple and be truthful, because if you kid yourself, you are only kidding yourself...

	Brand 'YOU'
Product Offerings (What are you 'selling'?)	
Characteristic Attributes (What people can always expect you to be!)	
Symbols & Signals (What colours, styles etc. are you known for?)	
Brand Personality (3 descriptors of your personality)	

History & Reputation (What reputation do you have? Baggage?)	
Associated Benefits (Functional, Emotional and/or Sensorial)	
Core Consumers (Who loves you the most?)	
Position / Role (Leader/Follower, father etc.)	
Brand Capsule (What is your Consumer's core idea of YOU in 3 words?)	

Once you have completed the quick take, share it with your key consumers – your boss, your spouse or significant other, and a few close friends who you can trust to give you honest feedback – firm it up and lock it down. If there are areas that you find you are not happy with, figure out what you would like those areas to say... we will figure out how to make that happen in the coming chapters.

A few tips on how to approach your quick take.

Be tough on yourself. If you find weaknesses, or 'areas of opportunity" as they are often euphemistically referred to as, recognize them for what they are, so that you can fix them over time. Ignoring them won't make them go away anyway.

If you find strengths – and there will be some! – note them down so that you can build on them. Those are your leverage points – they will come in very handy as you are building your brand identity, and trying to move forward with strengthening your personal brand.

CHAPTER 10

Your "consumer" & the "categories" you play in (how is this a source of advantage for you?)

What are you? In marketing terms, into what category of product do you fall? Who do you compete WITH for the rewards that you seek? To make it easier to understand, let's use McDonald's as an example. McD's is a fast food brand. So is Burger King. So, what are you?

For example... Athlete? Banker? Pediatrician? Plumber? Ad executive? That's easy, you say? Well, here are some things to think about.

1. **The categories you choose must be in consumer terms** – e.g. to your spouse, the categories might be husband, handyman, father to your kids, and so on. To your boss, they might be analyst, chief cook and bottle washer, accountant, sales person, or whatever. And to your friends, the categories might be completely different – support mechanism, designated driver, chess wizard or music aficionado.

2. **You – and your brand – will likely fit into multiple categories.** Understand that, embrace it, and manage it.

3. **Know with whom you are competing in each of your roles.** In the office, it's fairly clear. You and your co-workers are vying for the attention and praise of your boss. Right? Well, once you are properly branded, you stop competing on the stupid things, and start competing where it really matters – on your terms.

4. **Choose the category that suits you best.** That's right, you get to choose the category that suits your unique strengths and allows you to position yourself for the most flattering exposure, in the best light possible. This takes some creativity and thought, but if you are able to define the category properly, you become the only – and therefore the default – option. A classic example is the way Apple computers chose to define the category they play in – personal computers. They divided the world into two types of people – PC users and Mac users. How powerful is that? Just brilliant. So how do you find the perfect category for you? It's simple, but not easy. Define it in such a way that makes it impossible for it to be anyone BUT you.

So, take a few minutes and think about the four points above. How do you want to define yourself relative to everyone else? That is the beginning of true differentiation, and the source of your greatest strength as a brand.

Now, let's talk about **who you are competing FOR – your consumer... their hearts, their minds, and in many cases, their wallets.** You want to be first and foremost in your consumers' mind, right? So when your boss has a problem, he turns to you first. When he or she has to let people go from their team, who do they never even consider axing? When your spouse has issues, to whom does he or she turn to first? Your children? Your friends?

You need to truly understand your consumer to have any chance at dominating their thoughts and actions in any given area. And more importantly, recognize that knowledge is not absolute, it is relative. If you know your boss better than the other members of their team, that is a source of competitive advantage for you... but if you don't, then it puts you at a disadvantage.

What about your spouse? Do you know him or her better than anyone else? How many marital infidelities occur and long and otherwise 'healthy' marriages end because one person "doesn't understand" the other in the relationship? I'm sure you know someone who's life has been thus affected... if it's important to you, if this person, your spouse or significant other is truly a "consumer" in your life, you NEED to know them well, better than anyone else does, and they and everyone else in your life needs to acknowledge that.

So remember – **knowing your consumer really, really well is a source of competitive advantage for you.** Or it can be. And if you don't know them as well as someone else, you could seriously lose out. Here's how to ensure that does not happen.

The consumers in your landscape – even the ones that really matter – are unique. They have completely different needs, wants and desires. Different genders, different ethnicities, different ages, different lifecycle stages... so different. Yet these things are easily recognizable and it's hard to build a true understanding of a book by looking at its cover. So, you need to go deeper. You need to understand their values, their habits and their self-image, because these things drive the perceptions that drive their behaviour. In order to get the behaviour you are looking for – e.g. that raise or promotion from your boss – you need to understand the perceptions that you have to create in your boss's mind to make that happen. He has to believe that you are the best candidate for the job, the ideal candidate... in fact, the obvious and only choice.

Our perceptions are driven by our values, and those, along with our self-image, create the habits that we live our lives by. Here's how to build a deep understanding of your consumers – and you should answer these questions for all your key consumers, but at the very least, for your boss, your spouse, your family and your friends.

1. **What do they do in life to express who they are? What do they care about?** You need to understand their passions, their hobbies, and their interests, and not with a cynical view either. Remember, you are trying to truly understand what makes this person tick.

2. **How involved are they in your life?** Are they 'into' you, and what do they do to reflect that? Do they like to spend time with you? Are your interactions positive or negative?

3. **What do you mean to them? What is your role in their life?** Are you the chief whipping boy on your boss's staff, the guy who gets lumped with the worst assignments? Are you the spouse's true valentine?

4. **What triggers them to think of you?** Are you the go-to person in times of difficulty? The person your child turns to for comfort? When do they turn to you? Or not...

5. **What criteria must a replacement for you meet in order to be considered?** I know that's cold, but heck, how many people do you know that have been replaced overnight by someone younger, smarter, more qualified, and less expensive than the person being replaced? I bet you can think of one or two

people who fit that description... and this happens in business and in our personal lives. Ask yourself the tough questions now, and you may save yourself a great deal of unnecessary soul-searching later on...

6. **What behaviour, attitude or belief would cause them to reject you, or someone else, entirely?** For example, if you continually display a chauvinistic attitude towards the women in your life, you may end up without a spouse or a job. Which would be worse, I wonder?

7. **What type of people do these consumers tend to gravitate to?** Who do they identify with? Are you that type of person? If you don't even know with whom they want to be, you can't answer that with any certainty.

8. **How important are you in the lives of your consumer? Is their importance in your life matched by your importance in theirs?** While the balance is seldom exactly equal, it should at least be in the same ballpark; otherwise you are doomed in the long term.

9. And at the end, **demographics do matter.** If the age difference between you and your boss is 25 years (you are the older one), the chances of increased levels of strife and discord are higher. It makes the answers to all the above questions even more important for

you as you try to build a real understanding of your consumer... so that you can do an even better job of being the unique and differentiated brand that they choose every day, every time.

So, let's assume that you are on your way to building a deep understanding of what motivates and drives your consumer, and the attitudes, values and beliefs that they hold. Let's get to work putting together a powerful perception plan that can get them to believe what you want them to believe about you – so that you can get that next promotion, land the big job, or marry the girl of your dreams. And in case you were wondering, that's actually the easy part... ☺ It's much harder to bring that to life through your action plan, but there's no need to worry. We will get there together. Read on.

CHAPTER 11

Building Your Brand Funnel™ (your perception plan!)

In the world of marketing and brand development, there are a hundred different models used by companies around the world to create, build & manage the way their brands are perceived.

They all have certain elements in common, though, and these are the elements that you need to understand and focus on to build your own brand equity.

1. **It all starts and ends with the Brand Capsule.** The true essence of a brand, distilled down to three or four words. Every true brand has a capsule, and we know many of them without even realizing that in fact, the words themselves represent the truth behind the brands. For example... If I say the word 'Nike' to you, chances are you will say "Just Do It!"... Or you may even make a gesture with your hand that resembles a tick mark, or swoosh... and that would be enough for someone to understand everything you need him or her to get about the brand. What about Coke? "Happiness". Mont Blanc? "I'm

a success!" It works the other way around, too. "The Safe Car" will always be Volvo. Remember, this does not mean that BMW, Mercedes, Lexus or other car manufacturers are not safe – it's just that their brands stand for other things in the consumers' minds... So, what is your capsule? Start thinking about those few words that might be the essence of YOU. If you can't identify it in a positive and unique way, chances are no one else can, either. You will see why this is really important as you read on.

2. Arguably the **most important element of a perception plan is the Brand Positioning.** This is how brands build their uniqueness, and make clear how they stand out from their competition. The Brand Positioning answers four major questions:
   a. Who is the product for? (Your target market...)
   b. What type of product is it? (How is it categorized?)
   c. What benefit does it offer? (What itch do you scratch for them?)
   d. Why should anyone believe you? (No, really!)

In your case, you need to really define your audience - based on a deep understanding of their needs – and then figure out your true uniqueness. This is the thing that makes you special, your gift, your talent... but in order to build and sustain meaningful relationships with your target audience, this uniqueness has to be meaningful to them – a true benefit to them. We will talk a lot more about this in Chapter 13, but start thinking about what makes you unique. And if you can't think of at least one thing, don't worry ... it'll come to you! Or we will make one come true before this book is done ;)

3. **The product is the third piece of the perception plan – the tangibles that the brand delivers.** Coke will always own the stylized font that its name is written in, the red colour in which it is written (called Coca-Cola Red!), even the shape of the bottle is instantly recognizable, even if the bottle is nothing more than a pile of broken shards... So – what are the tangible reflections of you? The way you dress, obviously. Hair & make-up, yes. Accessories, perhaps even more so. Pretty much everything about you that another person – particularly your target audience - can sense with one of their five senses. So that includes your choice of soaps, shampoos, fragrances and so on. Think about how your tangibles are building or hurting the brand that is YOU.

4. **The fourth piece of the puzzle that is a brand's perception plan is – it's heritage.** Where does the brand come from? Where are its roots? So, when it comes to brand YOU,

this hardly needs any explanation, right? Well, its not that simple, because sometimes we tend to play down what makes us unique so that we can fit in better, and nowhere is that more true than in our heritage. How many Hispanics speak 'American' with a stronger accent than others because they believe it's the only way to fit in? What in your background makes you unique? Is it your ethnicity? Your language? Skin colour? The way you were raised, or where? Until you are ready to embrace that which makes you different – and hence unique – you are missing out on a great opportunity to brand yourself even more strongly.

5. **A critical – and sometimes ignored - piece of the Brand Funnel™ is the Brand Personality & Values.** Think of your favourite brand. Now imagine that brand is a person, and about to walk through the door. What do they look like? Male or female? Old or young? Educated or not? Urban or rural? Give them a personality and values, just like you would a real person. Now, take a step back and look at yourself. What are the top three personality attributes that you display, or are well known for? What values do you hold dear? These are not superficial things we are trying to get to here... these are the bedrock of your personality, the things that you can not, or choose not to, live without. Go deep. These are those aspects of you that you

are not going to be YOU without. Conversely, these things make YOU... YOU.

6. So, looking at the areas above, we come to **the Key Differentiators of a brand. These are the things that make any brand unique, and they can be drawn from any area of the above five.** In fact, if any brand hopes to succeed in the long-term, it needs to know what those differentiators are, and learn how to leverage them to the max. So... what your key differentiators? Which of the five areas of the Brand Funnel™ make you unique?

Are you ready to start building your own Brand Funnel™? Let's get started!

CHAPTER 12

The Brand Capsule (the top-of-mind idea you own)

Let's get into it.

If you were to sneak in to your target consumer's room in the middle of the night and wake up that poor, sleepy and bemused person and yell your name in their face – what will they yell or mumble back at you?

Think about that for a minute. (By the way, please don't actually try this exercise on any of your stakeholders – it's a theoretical exercise ☺ I suppose you might try it with your spouse or significant other, but you do risk being sent to the doghouse or worse...)

So, you yell your name at them. What do they say back?

Your capsule – the essence of what they remember, believe and think about you – is what they spit back. It's what they can access right away, and play back at you. It's unvarnished, boiled down, the essence of what you represent to them.

It's easy when we talk about brands, right?

"The cool computer."	Apple
"The real cola."	Coke
"Internet search."	Google

But does it work that well when we talk about people as brands? Let's take a look...

Mohammed Ali (Cassius Clay)	"Floats like a butterfly"...
Pele	"The greatest soccer player ever"...
Steve Jobs	"The creative genius behind Apple"...
Richard Branson	"The maverick CEO of Virgin"...

But these are world famous celebrities, you say. How can I hope to emulate these guys? Well, take a look around your circle of friends and family, colleagues & co-workers.

They all have certain views about you. Do you know how they see you? I mean really know? The challenge is – each major group of stakeholders will have a different capsule for you – if they have one at all.

BTW, they probably will have one, but it may not be the one you imagine, or wish for.

E.g. **To your spouse or significant other, you might be**

"The best hubby ever", or

"The best mother to my kids!", or even

"Bob the Builder"...

And how about "My cash machine" ☺

To your kids, you might be

"The best dad/mom ever", or

"My dad the math expert", or

"My mom the best cook", or

"My dad the car nut"...

To your co-workers, you could be

"The accounting whiz",

"The go-to guy in the team", or

"The royal suck-up"...

And to your boss, your capsule might be

"My wing man", or

"My go-to guy for any client issue", or

"The top ranked sales rep in the country"...

Do you see how challenging this is? Trying to come up with a capsule that you can own is very difficult – and it needs to be ownable because otherwise your replacement can very easily step into your shoes – literally & metaphorically. The challenge is that while your capsule may be different – or at least appear to be - for each one of your stakeholders, it needs to be rooted in a set of values & beliefs that is consistent, and credible and again – ownable by you.

Now, while you think about your capsule – those critical two or three words that represent the essence of YOU – let's move on and figure out how we are going to differentiate ourselves in the mass of humanity that we are competing with. We will come back to the capsule later, once you have gone through the rest of the process.

Remember, this is a process, and you may need to go through the cycle a couple of times to get to a point where you have something that you are comfortable building the rest of your life on. It will pay off.

On to the next step – developing a brand positioning that will set you apart and set you up for success.

CHAPTER 13

Positioning (how are you positioned against competition and what's your strategy to WIN?)

A brand's competitive positioning is the foundational discipline upon which the brand's identity is built. It highlights the **source of the brand's advantage – the source of its differentiation.**

It is the brand's unique promise in comparison to competition...

The brand positioning answers the consumer's four big questions with regards to any brand:

1. What kinds of people use it?

2. What kind of thing is it?

3. What makes it the one for me?

4. Why should I believe that?

A positioning statement looks like this:

To the (Core Target Market),

Brand X is the (Frame of Reference)

That delivers (an Owned Benefit)

Because (Reason to Believe)...

Let's see if you can guess what brand this positioning statement is for:

"For those who do creative things with computers,
Brand ＿＿＿＿＿ is
The computer brand
That's their creative partner
Because it is easy to use, and very, very cool."

If you guessed Apple, you were right. In fact, this positioning could not be true for any other brand. Therein lies its power. Now do you understand the power of a truly differentiated positioning?

Let's try another one.

"For those planning a vacation the whole family will love,
Brand ＿＿＿＿＿ is
The theme park
That pleases the child in everyone
Because it is a magical world of characters that they love."

Could it be any other park than Disney? No, not by a long shot.

So, the next question is – can this be applied to a person? Well, let's see if you can figure out who this is?

"For those people sick of the right wing conservative media with its clearly defined agenda,
_____ is
The must-watch political pundit / satirist
Who uses well-researched & scathing humour to expose the foibles & follies of those who would take America down a conservative, right wing path
Because his unique delivery, style, East Coast sensibilities & unerring sense of humour make his show the most-watched in its segment and great fun to boot!

Who could this be? Well, if you guessed Jon Stewart, the erstwhile host of the late night Daily Show on Comedy Central, you would be right? Could it be anyone else?

How about this person?

"For those who enjoy liberal political views and a heavy dose of satire in their political commentary,
_____ is
The 'faux conservative' political pundit
Who plays a self-obsessed, ultra-conservative, right wing, 'job creator' on his show

Because he can make his point most effectively while keeping his audience in splits the entire time.

Anyone? It's Steven Colbert (pronounced Col-berr as you well know :) of course. Who else could it be?

Those who are affiliated with these 'brands' would be able to tell you many, many things about them. What do people affiliated with you say? What does your brand's positioning look like?

There are some rules of positioning that you need to be aware of:

1. **If you are going to 'compete' in a particular category, you need to deliver on the 'cost-of-entry' factors in the category.** E.g. if you want to be known as the go-to guy in the Finance team, you better be hot stuff in Finance. If you want to be Dad #1, then you will need to invest the time with, and put out the love to, your family - that leads to being awarded this highest of honours.

2. **After you have delivered on the 'cost-of-entry', realize that you can't differentiate yourself on this.** This is simply a factor you have to deliver on just to be considered. If you are not capable of running the hundred metres in 10-11 seconds, don't even bother trying to compete in the category of "world-class sprinters"... as an example.

3. **Whoever is considered the leader in your chosen category, owns all the perceptions related to that category.** For example, if one of the moms on your block is currently regarded as "Best Mom", she will automatically be seen as the most caring mom, the one most likely to go the extra mile for her kids. If that's you – great. If its not, and you want it to be, recognize that you will need to find a different Brand Essence to own.

4. **You cannot be all things to all people.** Its simply not possible, and the sooner you recognize that, the better off you will be.

5. **Anyone trying to take on the mantle of leadership has to position relative to the leader.** If you are the leader in your particular category, realize that everyone else is positioning relative to you.

6. You know the old adage **"You don't get a second chance to make a first impression"? Well, it's absolutely true.** The first impression is also the last impression – and it is terribly difficult to change. So put some thought into your positioning – it is a long-term decision, with really long-term ramifications.

7. And last but not least – **every way the brand – YOU – touches your consumer must be consistent with the Brand Positioning. Inconsistency is Death.**

Remember, the brand positioning answers the four big questions with regards to any brand:

1. What kinds of people use it?

2. What kind of thing is it?

3. What makes it the one for me?

4. Why should I believe that?

Before we start detailing each of these areas together, let's take a step back and decide what your overall strategy options are. This is straight from the war manuals of Sun Tzu, and others. It is deep. Think it through. After all, it is your future we are talking about.

Let's go on.

CHAPTER 14

What's your positioning strategy?

There are six major positioning strategies that are generally available to brands in today's hyper-competitive world. They can work equally well for Brand YOU.

1. Remain the leader

If you own something unique and sustainable in the hearts & minds of your audience – never let it go. Even if it goes out of fashion, or becomes less popular for some reason... Don't abandon it, instead build on it. You can shape it, redirect it – but walking away from it is not even possible, even if it were desirable. No, own it – really own it. Make it yours, so that no one can take it away from you. E.g. If you are the go-to person in the sales support team that the entire sales team relies on for timely and accurate data – BE that person. Embrace it. Build on it to branch out into new areas of expertise that you can also bring in to your 'franchise'.

2. Take the leader head-on

For the record, strategy #2 is rarely recommended, because if you try and take away the leadership mantle from someone by trying to stand for the exact same thing that they stand for – you will end up strengthening their position, and they will not even bother to thank you for it. The only time this works is when you can demonstrate a tangible, ownable benefit that is currently not being offered – and deliver that benefit with a bang that you can own. E.g. If you want to be seen as 'the power finance guy' in your outfit, but this capsule currently belongs to someone else, you will need to do something major to take that mantle from them. Go back to school. Get another degree. It will require a major investment, and there are sometimes better and faster ways of achieving similar results. BTW, I'm not for one second recommending that you NOT invest in continuing education – I think it is a must in today's competitive environment, and is one the few enduring sources of competitive advantage you can own – truly own. But sometimes, there are practical reasons that prevent you from going back to school immediately. Don't lose heart – there is always another way.

3. Assault the leader's relative weakness

Every leader, no matter how powerful, how strong, has an Achilles' heel. A weakness. If you can find that, you can exploit it to create a powerful positioning strategy for yourself that will endure – and really help you to differentiate yourself in the long-term. E.g. If the capsule you are trying to own is 'Best Dad Ever!' and it is currently owned by a neighbour who seems to do everything right, invest some time to study the real needs of your 'consumers' – your kids. Do they really need you to be buying them stuff? Or would they prefer that you take out an hour in the evening to play outdoors with them? How important is that to you? Can you come home at 5pm to be able to do that? How about making it a point to go out camping with the kids on the weekend – even if it is only in the back yard? Once you find the thing that your neighbour is not doing, despite being seen as Dad #1, and start doing it with heart, consistently, you will find that you will soon become that person and own the capsule that you are looking for.

4. Take a vulnerable target market

Find a consumer group that the current leader is not speaking to, not appealing to, and speak to them in a way that they 'get' you, and truly understand the benefit that you bring to the table versus anyone else. E.g. If there is already a 'go-to' person for the sales team to turn to, is there another group of under-served 'customers' that you can impress with your work, your credentials, and your attitude? Perhaps your own team? Perhaps the operations team? Who knows how many people or groups of people are not currently aware of your abilities, your amazing skills? Find a new group and wow them.

5. Turn the tables

If the capsule you want – or are angling for – is owned by someone else, here's another strategy that can be quite effective. Find the source of their strength, and turn it into a weakness. E.g. If someone works 24/7, that can be construed as a person incapable of achieving work-life balance. A person who leaves on the dot at 5pm – because they have a life – can be presented as someone unwilling to go the extra mile for your boss (your number one customer at work, remember?)... And so on.

6. Open new territory

Sometimes, despite all your best efforts, your unceasing attempts to differentiate yourself go unanswered and unrewarded. At that point, it is time to change the game. Whether it involves leaving an unappreciative boss, or getting out of a negative relationship, the decision to get out is always a difficult and sometimes painful one. Remember this – there will always be a situation out there that works better for you. Keep looking. Don't compromise. Life is too short to be unappreciated and unrewarded – and underpaid. Find what you are good at – what your real identity is – and be that person.

Be the brand.
You can do it.

CHAPTER 15

Who is your target market? (Pick the one that suits you best!)

Your target market is the people that you – the product – are designed to please. Who is it that you are doing all this for? If you are a psychopathic personality (according to the clinical definition), then that is a small audience of one. You. And just so you know, between 4% and 6% of the world population fits the definition of psychopaths ☺

And BTW, CEOs in today's corporate world are four times as likely to fit that profile. Are you surprised, given the callous & uncaring behaviour that we have seen, and continue to witness today?

So, assuming that you are not a psychopathic personality, which group of people are you trying to influence? How are you the solution that this audience is looking for – the 'itch' that they 'need' to scratch?

There are **three major criteria that you can use to decide who your target audience should be:**

1. **A meaningful identity.** If you defined the audience properly, and read them the definition you wrote, would they recognize

themselves – and would they care? Would they say – 'Hey, that's me!" You can't give a generic definition of this identity – something like 'the boss that wants the best from their employees' – because that is every boss. It can't be that general...

To know if you have indeed developed a meaningful identity for your audience, you can use what we call the "Window Test". If you were to climb up to the 10th floor of a building on a busy street and yell down to the street below – "Hey, all mothers who want the best nutrition for my children!" – the chances are you would attract all the women above a certain age. That's no good. If on the other hand, you said something along the lines of – "Hey, all those who want to motivate, excite and drive their team to new heights of achievement!" – well, you would certainly get a different group, wouldn't you?

Similarly, if you defined your target audience as "senior management" – that would probably be too broad. On the other hand, a more meaningful identity might be along the lines of "forward-thinking, tech-savvy, members of the senior management team who are devoted to building the technical backbone of your company"... now that's a different bunch. Might be the same people – just defined differently. And I humbly submit – more meaningfully for you and for them!

2. **Motivation.** Does the definition you wrote clearly contain the itch that needs to be scratched – and show how YOU are going to scratch it – the unique benefit YOU offer? Let's take a look at Jon Stewart. Implicit in all that he does and says is the clear benefit to you, the viewer, that he will take a certain point of view about the hot button topics of the day. You tune in – or tune out – for that exact reason! You appreciate – or not – his take on topics as varied as the Republican primaries, the situation in the Middle East or the peccadilloes of certain politicians, some of whom may or may not be his friends.

What about Richard Branson, the charismatic (despite being slightly crazy or perhaps, because of it!) chairman of the Virgin group of companies? Why do people – especially media and members of the press – turn out in droves for one of his events? Because he can be guaranteed to do something that will be newsworthy – that is the unique benefit he offers to the 24-hour news cycle. And boy, does he deliver column centimeters ☺ usually with gripping visuals!

3. **Mass – is the target market you offer this benefit to as big (or small) as it needs to be?** You don't want to restrict yourself, but you don't want to go too wide either. At the same time, you want the category of people in your target market to want to be a part

of the market – the way you have defined it. They need to want to be a part of the club – the exclusive club – that you are inviting them to – and they should be proud to be associated with it.

Who wouldn't want to be a part of these groups?

"Those with the guts to push themselves past their own limits!"

"Executives who have earned the power that prestige brings!"

"Career women who know how to be a great mom!"

So – who is your target audience? Think about how you are going to define them to your maximum advantage...

CHAPTER 16

With whom are you competing? (You get to decide your frame of reference!)

Who are you competing with in your professional and personal lives?

By the way, if you don't think you are competing with anyone, you are way too Zen for this book. Read no further. Relax. Take another chill pill. (Please note – I am not advocating pharmaceutical solutions of any sort!). Continue down the path you are on, and I hope to join you on that path in a few years (or not).

If on the other hand, you recognize that – whether you like it or not, and whether it is fair or not – you are in a competition, then let's continue.

Many times, it is not a fair competition. How many people do you know who have lost husbands to younger women? Been 'reorganized' out of jobs that have gone to younger people? What about parents dying alone, having lost relevance in the lives of their children, and their children's lives?

The good news is that the competitive sets we live with are not necessarily those that we were born with. You – YOU – can choose who you are going to compete with. If you do this properly – you can actually make your competition irrelevant.

An example of how a brand has done this effectively is Apple. An iconic brand, yes. But most importantly – there are only two types of computers in the world today, as far as the public is concerned. Apple – and PCs. In one fell swoop, Apple (through a concerted and focused effort) made all the other brands of PCs redundant. They basically said – either you are an Apple user, or you are not. If you are not, that's OK. But when you, Mr. or Mrs. User, are ready to graduate to Apple, we will be here for you...

In marketing terms, Apple redefined the Frame of Reference so that it works only for them. Powerful stuff.

So how do we make this work for you? Here's what you need to do.

1. **Start by reviewing your competitive landscape – your Frames of Reference - all the landscapes available to you.**

2. **Determine the Frame of Reference (FOR) you can win in – and that's worth winning in!**

3. **The Frame of Reference you choose must meet these criteria:**

a. **Simplicity:** "I know exactly who I'm competing with!" Is the Frame of Reference that you have chosen understandable by your 'consumer' without explanation or effort? Most importantly, does it answer the following three questions simply and directly:

i. **What ARE you?**

Father. Athlete. Accountant. Manager. Sales Rep. And so on.

ii. **What do you DO?**

Provide an amazing home environment. Run the 4-minute mile. Provide accurate financial statements. Run your team like a well-oiled machine. Exceed your targets every single quarter. And so on.

iii. **What Emotional Benefit do you provide?**

Always there for your children. Driven to excel on and off the track. Guaranteed to get the numbers right the first time. A job given to you is a job done. The go-to person in the sales team who always takes up the slack.

b. **Significance:** "I can demonstrate how the benefit I offer is unique, and stands out from the others in this group." Does the Frame of Reference you have chosen set up a meaningful differentiation?

Remember, every Frame of Reference you choose will automatically have both positive and negative associations that go with it. This is just the way it is. Embrace it.

For example, take the category of 'weight lifters'.

What are some of the positive associations that this category comes with? Strength. Muscles. Focus. Determination. Passion. Energy. Did I mention strength?

What about the negatives? Not very attractive to look at. Prone to injury. Linked to drug use & abuse. And so on.

So – understand well the FOR you choose – think it through because it will stay with you once you define it for your 'consumer' to see, and invite them to view you in that light.

c. **Scale:** The Frame of Reference should be as large as the other two will allow. Remember, a bigger scale is not necessarily better. The issue is that of the 'Zone of Authority' (ZOA). How far does your ZOA stretch? It is often better to succeed as a power player in a smaller category – be a big fish in a small pond – than try to play in a category that is unnecessarily large...

And don't forget to consider direct and indirect competition – many a brand has been knocked off its perch by competition that it never even saw coming. For example, the biggest selling camera in India a couple of years ago was actually Nokia – not Nikon, or Canon, or any other 'actual' camera brand. Do you think they saw it coming?

So. What is your frame of reference? Where in your world can YOU best compete & with whom do you compete? **On what benefit can YOU win?** Do you know? If not, well, you'd better find out.

CHAPTER 17

Owning a powerful benefit (what is the 'itch' that only Brand YOU can scratch for your consumer?)

What is a benefit? A paycheck? A social service cheque? Unemployment payments? How about a bonus payment at the end of the year? Yes, these are benefits of a sort. But the type of benefit we are talking about is different. What benefit do YOU – the brand – offer to your consumers?

The benefit we are talking about is the consumer's real reward that they get from your being a part of their lives. It goes much beyond money, a home, food and clothing, toys and other 'things'. They can get those things elsewhere. Sometimes, they can get much more elsewhere – hence the high divorce rate prevalent in society today.

No, we are talking about providing a real scratch for an itch that the consumer has – and you are the scratcher. We are talking about the result of a deep understanding of what your consumer – your boss, your family, your co-workers – need and are currently missing in their lives, and being able to fill that gap, scratch that itch for them in such a way that the result is nothing short of a gigantic AAAAHHHHH for them.

Are you with me? Good. But, how do you go about building your 'owned benefit'?

Start by reviewing your capsule. What was the core idea there? You have to push past the simple descriptive features of what you offer – these can be replicated and matched easily enough. No, you need to offer real benefits, and there are three types of benefits that you can offer:

1. **Functional Advantage**
   a. Brand X - 'Helps you go longer, stronger...'
   b. Brand Y - 'Strengthens the digestive tract!'
   c. Brand YOU – 'Makes sure his family has the best lifestyle money can buy!"

2. **Emotional Payoff**
   a. Brand X - 'You will feel primed to pounce on every opportunity!'
   b. Brand Y – 'It will give you wings!'
   c. Brand YOU – 'Stands by her spouse through thick and thin!'

3. **Experiential Reward**
   a. Brand X - 'You'll feel that second wind kick in...'
   b. Brand Y - 'Tastes like a blast of cold Rocky Mountain air...'
   c. Brand YOU – 'When I delegate a task to her, I have total peace of mind because I know it's going to be done!'

Your owned benefit must meet the following criteria:

1. **Is it Desirable: "I want that!"**

   No explanation should be required. It should answer the simple question – 'What's in it for me?'

2. **Is it Deliverable: "I can tell this person can do what they say"**

   Will the consumer see the promise as being fulfilled? Don't disappoint your consumers... you will lose them!

3. **Is it Defensible: "Only this person owns this, and it is unique to them"**

   Can you own the association? It must be seen as your promise, and nobody else's!

Remember – the benefit you own must be singular. The old adage of "you can't be all things to all people" is never more true than here. Choose carefully.

A quick look at the technical difference between a Feature, a Function & a real Benefit might be helpful at this stage, as you start to work out your unique owned benefit, because the sad thing is that even seasoned marketers sometimes get this wrong.

1. **Feature: a descriptive fact – something a product HAS.**

    E.g. The car you drive, the suit you wear, the accessories you carry.

2. **Function: an operational advantage – something a product does.**

    E.g. The charities you support, the job you do, the sports you play.

3. **Benefit: the real reward from the features & functions.**

    E.g. the real itch that you scratch for your consumer, which comes from what kind of a person you are, the values you hold. That makes you the father you are, the boss, the co-worker and the colleague.

Let me introduce you to Maslow's hierarchy of needs. In 1943, psychologist Abraham Maslow postulated a theory that has come to be central to helping marketers understand consumer behaviour as it pertains to brands. It basically says that there are five stages of needs that all human beings evolve through:

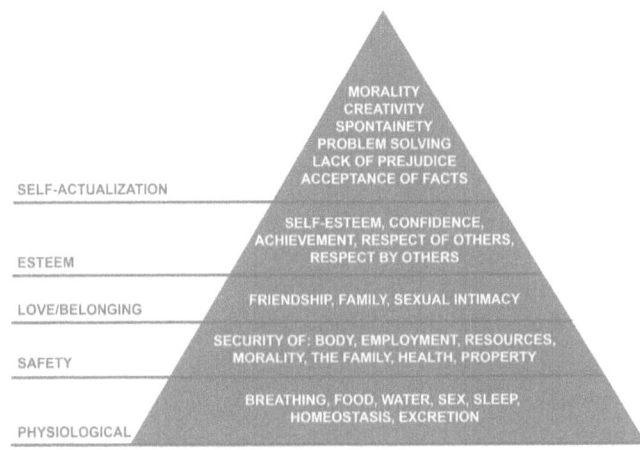

The hierarchy helps us to understand the way our needs – and those of our target consumers - develop and evolve over time, and in different situations. Why is this important? Because the benefit we offer our consumer has to answer that need – and any tool that can help us to reach a better understanding of needs and need states must be used!

Basically, the model says that until basic physiological needs – food, water, shelter etc. – are met, we cannot worry about higher level needs, such as health, friendship, self-esteem or overcome our prejudices... indeed, the hierarchy is a very powerful tool to help us understand ourselves and our reactions in various situations as well.

Look at the hierarchy – what happens when one level of needs is not met? Is it possible for someone to be successful in love when he or she is concerned about his or her safety and wellbeing?

So, if you are to be successful in offering a true benefit to your consumer, you need to truly understand your consumers' as well as possible. Since we are talking about multiple consumers, you need to really dig deep and build a broad-based understanding that will stand you in good stead as you try to offer benefits that make you irreplaceable in the lives of those people.

Another useful tool is called the **"mental mirror"**. Here's how it works:

HOW DO THEY FEEL NOW?	HOW ARE YOU MAKING THEM FEEL?
Sheepishly confused by the complexity of financial documents	Publicly confident with the ease of the numbers as explained by you, their go-to person for accounting enigmas
Defeated & lost because of the flu	Calm and relaxed, resting in bed, knowing that everything will be alright
Exhausted & bitter from lack of sleep because the baby is teething, and crying all night	Positively refreshed by the respite that you bring by staying up all night with the baby
Dejected by the onset of old age	Jubilant at the way you make them feel

Take your time with this. Identifying the real benefit Brand YOU offers, or are going to offer is central – and vital - to your long-term success.

CHAPTER 18

I am make a difference

I'm different!

RTB (Reason-To-Believe – why should anyone buy what you're selling?)

In an ideal world, you wouldn't need an RTB – a reason for people to accept the unique brand that is YOU. They would simply see YOU for what you are – an invaluable, irreplaceable part of their lives.

Unfortunately, that is often not the way it is. People can be quite cynical sometimes, especially when the new Brand Identity you have developed and are trying to bring to life is a significant deviation from what you have demonstrated and owned in the past. At least initially, it will need some convincing – and a good Reason-To-Believe can be essential part of your new Brand ID.

If you can do without, please do. If you can't, then remember to keep it simple. Ask yourself if your consumer will demand 'proof' of what you have promised – the benefit you will deliver. If the answer is "Yes", then choose the simplest proof that is directly related to the benefit – and the key word is 'simple'.

There are three major criteria to keep in mind when selecting a powerful RTB:

1. **Is it plausibly unique?**

   Is it unique, first? If not, then it could be hard to own. For example: 'dependable'. You might indeed embody this trait, but can you own it entirely? And second, is it uniquely true about YOU? Only YOU? If it isn't, then it may not work. Now if you can tweak it so that 'dependable' becomes something more, then it might be more powerful. "Never misses a ball game". "Never fails to deliver insightful commentary that is bound to have you in stitches." And so on.

2. **Is it persuasive?**

   Does the Reason to Believe that you have come up with really 'prove' the benefit? Will your consumer nod his or her head upon hearing this and say – yes, I get that! If not, probably needs a bit of re-thinking. Remember, if it is needed at all, it must be convincing, or it is worse than useless.

3. **Is it a 'put-away' shot?**

   Does it nail the positioning as YOURS? Is it a slam-dunk? Again, if it isn't, then perhaps don't bother with it at all. Because this is your final attempt to convince someone of the benefit of starting / continuing to engage with your brand, and after this, there is nothing else left in your arsenal. It better work.

Where can you find a "Reason To Believe" that meets the criteria above? Here are some possible areas:

1. **Is there something about you that is unique – anything?** How about your heritage? Ethnicity? Education? Experience? Character? Personality? Passions? All or any of these might make an interesting start point. Remember, what and who you are IS actually unique – and if you are struggling to find a uniqueness, its only because you have never actually looked at yourself in this way before. Also, if you are struggling to define your own uniqueness – guess how hard it must be for someone else to identify what makes you into a brand worthy of attention and engagement?

2. **What are your passions?** What do you believe in, strive for, and drive towards? Are you a scoutmaster? A calligrapher? A football coach for the local primary school? These passions can provide a unique and compelling RTB that supports the benefit you are trying to own.

3. **Who are the people that choose to be with you – choose your 'brand' – and why?** Do they 'get' the benefit that you want to offer

and own, or is it for other reasons? E.g. do you want people to acknowledge you for your creativity – but the real reason that they hang with you is that you are wealthy and can spend money fecklessly when you are with them? Or are you striving to be recognized for your accounting skills – but the boss only sees you as someone safe to flirt with (because you might not openly reject him / her for fear of consequences).

So, in a nutshell – have an RTB only if you must have one. Having said that, if your desired Brand Identity requires a significant departure from the Identity you currently have (not the one you THINK you have) then you will almost certainly need a powerful Reason To believe. And it better be a slam-dunk.

Because after you present your RTB, that's it… if your target audience still doesn't buy into Brand YOU, then they are probably never going to. Let's hope that it doesn't come to that, but if it does, I will do my best to help you re-evaluate the work you have done so far, and get you on the right track. My e-mail is omar@brandhotline.com. Hopefully, you won't need it, but if you do, I'm here to help.

CHAPTER 19

Putting together your competitive positioning (3 parts, 1 thought!)

The positioning statement has three parts – the core target (your audience), the frame of reference (your competitive set) and the benefit (what you offer).

So, how do you know if the statement you have is a good one?

Here are some criteria that can help you evaluate whether the statement that you have built does in fact work:

1. **Is it cohesive?** (Does the statement hang together?)

2. **Is it credible?** (Is it reasonably believable?)

3. **Is it compelling?** (Does it offer something worth buying?)

4. **Is it capsulable?** (Can it be summed up succinctly; can it be nutshelled?)

So overall, if you want to check the quality of your work, here's a summary of the criteria we use:

Target Market	Meaningful Identity	Motivation	Mass
Frame of Reference	Significance	Simplicity	Scale
Owned Benefit	Desirable	Deliverable	Ownable
Reason To Believe	Plausible	Persuasive	"Put Away"
Whole Statement	Cohesive	Credible	Compelling
			... and CAPSULABLE!

There are some problems that you might face in writing the statement. E.g. don't put selling language in your frame of reference – try to be as descriptive as possible without selling yourself in this area. Try to avoid circular arguments – for example, putting your benefit in to your target audience descriptor usually is not helpful. But generally, if you have really put your mind to the tasks so far, the positioning statement should really come together nicely now.

What next? Product! (The tangibles Brand YOU always delivers!)

This is where your brand earns its positioning. Here we deal with those things that your "consumer" will experience with their five senses. So, how can you, the product, prove that you, the brand, are worthy of the positioning? Here are some useful areas to start considering:

1. **What are some adjectives that come to mind when you and other talk about you?** I.e. what is your product halo?

2. **What is the "stuff" about you that other people "consume"?**

3. **What does your "packaging" look like?**

4. **What are some of the "symbols" or "signals" that you are known for?**

Let's do a creative exercise here. I'd like you to design a logo for your brand based on the brand positioning that you have built in the last few chapters. This should be as "good" as you can make it. If you can afford to work with a professional designer, then do.

(BTW, this is not as expensive as you might think. There are quite a few web-based designers who will do a logo design for you for $100 or less.) If not, do it yourself; it's challenging but fun. Put some thought in to it. Like anything else, the more effort you put in to it, the better the result is likely to be.

But be careful. It does need some thought ☺

Start with a good look at your name. Most people are comfortable with their names, but many people never truly come to terms with theirs. Certain names in certain contexts lead to generalizations being made about you that are undesirable but unavoidable. The sooner you figure out how your name adds value to, or detracts from, your Bank of Brand Equity, the better off you will be. Of course, if you do a good job of owning it, then it almost doesn't matter what your name is – over time, or in an instant, it can become synonymous with what you stand for – or want to stand for.

But the product is YOU. Everything tangible about you – from your clothes to your makeup, your accessories to your personal hygiene, your preferred mode of transport to your degree of organization at work and at home. Anything that people can "experience" with their five senses. People say that 90% of communication is non-verbal (and that % may actually be higher than that). If that doesn't scare you, I don't know what does.

How many of us actually take the time to 'manage' our 'tangibles'? If you are an on-air personality, then of course you do. You have stylists and teams of PR people in place to manage the image of Brand YOU. But if you are Joe or Jane Professional trying to build a career, then generally you clean up as best as you can, and get out there hoping for the best.

If you agree that our first impression of people is made in the first few seconds of meeting them, then that approach is simply not going to cut it for Brand YOU.

Things that you need to take an objective look at, and evaluate through your own eyes, as well as the eyes of your 'target consumers':

1. Clothing / sense of style
2. Hair cut / hair style
3. Makeup
4. Accessories
5. Footwear
6. Personal grooming & hygiene
7. Handshake (the initial impression)
8. Inter-personal skills
9. Listening skills
10. Speech patterns (tonality, nasality, pronunciation etc.)
11. And so much more...

It might seems obvious that if you aspire to be a part of the senior management team in a large multinational corporation, then you might consider losing the blue hair and various pieces of metal in your face. If you do decide to keep them, then you shouldn't wonder why you never get promoted to management. I'm not saying it is good or bad – but **you have to dress/act the part that you are aspiring for.** You don't see too many CEOs or CFOs with over-the-top expressions of their personalities in their personal tangibles – and there is a reason for that. The exceptions, like Richard Branson, have a good reason for being exceptions – and let's face it, if you have decided that you want to model yourself on Branson, then that is a long and tough road that you have embarked on ☺. The maverick CEO is a much-desired Brand Image – and one that is notoriously hard to deliver on.

CHAPTER 21

The Heritage (where do you come from – and how does that help to differentiate you from the crowd?)

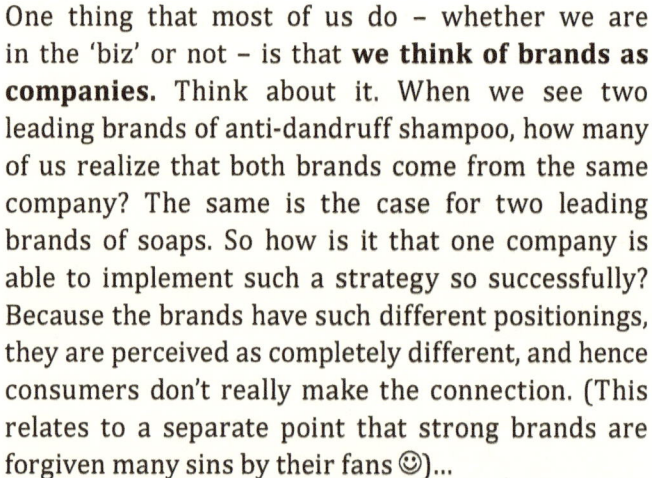

One thing that most of us do – whether we are in the 'biz' or not – is that **we think of brands as companies.** Think about it. When we see two leading brands of anti-dandruff shampoo, how many of us realize that both brands come from the same company? The same is the case for two leading brands of soaps. So how is it that one company is able to implement such a strategy so successfully? Because the brands have such different positionings, they are perceived as completely different, and hence consumers don't really make the connection. (This relates to a separate point that strong brands are forgiven many sins by their fans ☺)...

Most brands start out as entrepreneurial efforts – and guess who the entrepreneur behind YOUR brand is? If you said ME (referring to yourself) – you are correct. As mentioned earlier, you are also the CEO, CFO, CMO etc. etc.

So how do you go about defining your "heritage"? Some useful areas to consider are:

1. **Your mission!** What do you think you exist? Is there a purpose to your existence? If there is, what is it? If you don't know, then you really need to think about it. It's a tough question to answer, so give it the time that it deserves.

2. **What is your core expertise?** Do you have any unique capabilities that set you apart, that define you, that define the way you see the world? Try to look at it from the point of view of your "consumer". Is it something that they would be willing to "pay" for in some shape or form?

3. **Is there something special about the people you hang out with?** At work? At the gym? At your club? Are you an influencer in an online community? Our parents used to say that your friends define you – boy, were they right!

This is a deceptively challenging part of your Brand Identity. It must be done well, and it must be authentic and believable – and most importantly, it must make you more desirable to your 'consumer'.

CHAPTER 22

Personifying Brand YOU (seriously... figuring out WHO you want to be, focusing on Values & Personality)

One of the exercises that marketers find useful during market research is to try to get consumers to describe the brands that they like or dislike in terms of the people they might be. We call it Brand Personification. **"If your brand was a human being, and they walked through the door right now, they would look like..."** The answers you get in terms of male / female, young / old, educated / not, urban / rural, etc. are extremely interesting – and sometimes quite shocking to the Brand Manager. You see, **sometimes the person who is closest to the brand – the Brand Manager – is the one least able to see the brand objectively.**

I read somewhere that 99% of people who regularly drink either Pepsi or Coke believe that they can identify their brand by taste alone in a blind taste test. Less than 1% actually can. That's astonishing. But less so when you think about it...

You see where I'm going with this ☺.

You would think that it would be relatively easy for you to 'personify' your own brand. Like heck it is. **We** are, with very few exceptions, largely blind to our own imperfections, and yet we believe, some of us with entirely misplaced confidence, that we know ourselves like the proverbial backs of our hands. We don't.

So – how would you go about defining YOU as a person? We are looking for a real archetype, a clearly recognizable persona that people can and will identify with. The descriptors we are going to be looking for are way beyond 'friendly', 'fun-loving' or 'sociable'. These are more than just words – they will help define the relationship between you and your consumer(s), and the nature of the bond that you have.

Here's how it looks:

1. **The Archetype:** defines who YOU are to your consumer – and the role you play in their lives.

2. **Values:** three things YOU believe passionately.

3. **Personality:** three traits that YOU always exhibit.

These of course have to mirror the positioning you have defined for yourself – and help bring it to life.

Let's look at an example. Who is this?

1. The smart & funny liberal pundit who can be relied on to tell it like it is!

2. Values:
   a. The truth needs to be told
   b. Integrity above all else
   c. Humor drives home the point better

3. Exhibits:
   a. Passion for the truth
   b. A self-deprecating & irreverent sense of humour and
   c. An uncanny ability to frame the important issues of the day for the American (and global) public

Yes, Jon Stewart is the embodiment of this, his brand persona. This is what makes his show so compelling, and his Daily Show into such a powerful and globally recognized brand.

There are several steps you could take here.

Step 1: Write down your existing Persona as you see it today. Dig deep. Make it meaningful. Try to describe yourself in real terms, not how you think other people see you, but how you actually are. Can you write an archetype statement for yourself? What are your values – the things you believe in passionately? How would you describe your personality – those traits that make you who you are? Do you know what they are?

Step 2: Validate this with 'consumers' who know you well. I would suggest starting with your spouse or significant other, close friends, your boss and close colleagues. The easiest way to get this feedback is through a simple questionnaire designed to make it easy for your consumers to give you feedback in a safe and non-critical environment. A series of statements with a sliding scale (1-5 with 1 indicating complete disagreement and 5 indicating complete agreement) should be helpful.

E.g. I am innovative. I balance work and life well. I am trustworthy.

It depends on what values or personality traits you are asking about. Framing the statements properly will be critical. You should allow the respondents to add statements that they feel are reflective of your persona. That will ensure that all points of view are captured, and that the feedback you receive is more holistic than you might be able to ensure on your own. (Remember what we said earlier about the Brand Manager having potentially glaring blind spots when it comes to their own Brand?)

Step 3: Once you have the feedback collated (throw it in to a spreadsheet for easy tabulation), identify the gap between your perceptions and others' perceptions of you. Understand this gap. Internalize it. Even if the gap is vast and not entirely complimentary, accept it for what it is and move on to the next step. (This BTW is much easier said than

done but at some point you will need to BABAGOI –
Build A Bridge And Get Over It!).

Step 4: Write down your desired Persona –
complete with an Archetype, Values and Personality.
Remember, at this stage, don't focus too much on the
'how' you are going to achieve that, although a little
bit of grounding in reality is probably not a bad thing.

Now that this last critical piece of the Brand Funnel™
is done, you are now ready to put the entire Brand
Identity together.

CHAPTER 23

Putting your Brand Identity together (don't forget what differentiates you from anyone else!)

So far, we have been travelling through the Brand Funnel™ and we have built a capsule, a positioning, a heritage, product attributes and a brand persona for Brand YOU.

But there were 6 pieces to the Funnel if you refer back to where we started. **The 6ᵗʰ and final piece is the Key Differentiators.**

What are your Key Differentiators and where can they be found?

Review the work you have done on the Funnel so far. Keeping in mind the Brand Firedance, **select the 3-5 most powerful, differentiating and memorable associations that you can.** Ideally, each should trigger the others and together they should mean only one possible Brand – YOU!

These associations will be key in building your brand in the future. You will need to keep them in the forefront of your mind as you move forward to ensure that you are building your brand on a consistent platform.

So now it is time to put together your completed Brand Identity. Here is how it should look, and ideally you want it to fit on one page.

JON STEWART
Capsule: The brilliantly funny
American liberal pundit

Brand Positioning:
For those people sick of the right wing conservative
media with it's clearly defined agenda,
Jon Stewart is the must-watch
political pundit / satirist

That uses well-researched & scathing humour to expose the foibles & follies of those who would take America down a conservative, right wing path Because his unique delivery, style, East Coast sensibilities & unerring sense of humour make his show the most-watched in its segment, and great fun to boot!

Product Attributes
- Immaculate suit & tie
- Ability to do creative impressions (specially Old Jewish Grandmother from NY)
- Shorter than most people (and focuses on this with taller guests in typical self-deprecating style)

Heritage
- New York Jewish upbringing
- Over a decade of hard-hitting journalism
- Ownership of humour & satire as a weapon of truth

Personification
- **Archetype:** The smart & funny liberal pundit who can be relied on to tell it like it is!
- **Values**
o The truth needs to be told
    o Integrity above all else
    o Humor drives home the point better
- **Personality**
    o Passion for the truth

- A self-deprecating & irreverent sense of humour and
- An uncanny ability to frame the important issues of the day for the American (and global) public

Key Differentiators

- The brilliantly funny American liberal pundit
- His unique delivery, style, East Coast sensibilities & unerring sense of humour
- New York Jewish upbringing
- Ownership of humour & satire as a weapon of truth

Now that your Brand Perception plan – the Brand Identity – has been carefully laid out, it is time to start bringing Brand YOU! to life. Before you do that though, run it by your key consumers. See what they have to say. Ensure that at least your key consumers are fully aligned to where you are going – and then move forward with confidence knowing that you are on the right track.

CHAPTER 24

Bringing your Brand Identity to life – planning your communication strategy!

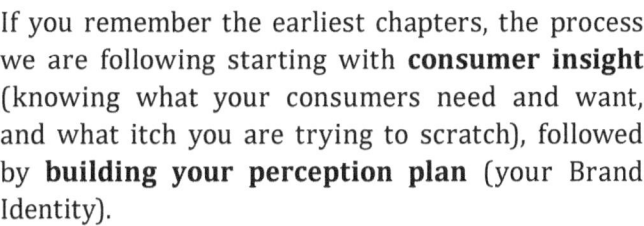

If you remember the earliest chapters, the process we are following starting with **consumer insight** (knowing what your consumers need and want, and what itch you are trying to scratch), followed by **building your perception plan** (your Brand Identity).

Now we start **breathing life into your Identity through a Marketing Mix that best tells the story of your brand.** The challenge here is that your consumers already have a perception of you, so if you are going to create a new perception, you need to get them to notice that there is something different about you. So you need to keep three things in mind as you try to communicate your new Brand Identity:

- **Disrupt:** In order for your consumer to actually notice a shift or departure from the norm, you have to disrupt the norm of your relationship dynamic. Think of it as a reboot – where new settings kick in and perceptions change.

- **Engage:** You need to engage with your consumers at the new level that you have decided upon in your perception plan. Once people start looking at you in this new light, half your job is done.

- **Convince:** As you embark on this journey, remember that every action you take is either a deposit into, or a withdrawal from, the bank of your brand equity. If you stay consistent to your new / improved Brand Identity, there should be little or no convincing required as you build towards your desired Equity.

As you think of this, keep in mind that Brand YOU! is just like any other brand. You need a communication plan that tells the story of Brand YOU! in a holistic way, and brings the brand alive for your target consumer in an engaging and interesting way. After all, **you want your target consumer to WANT to engage with Brand YOU!**

So... when is your target audience most likely to be open to seeing the new & improved YOU? In marketing jargon, we try to catch them when the clay is moist... when they are attentive, receptive and at a point of need. So when your boss comes to you with a new project, or is desperately looking for a point person on a major new assignment, that would be a good time to introduce them to the new YOU! Or when your spouse wants to 'talk', you actually switch off the TV and listen – without interruption. And then respond in a way that brings your new Brand Identity to life in a positive and recognizable way.

Is it possible to predict when your target will be receptive, so that you can be better prepared? I mean, it would be helpful to know just when to bring your new game, right? It would allow you to be more relaxed, and more focused on a better Brand YOU! Well, here's how you can figure out when the clay is more likely to be moist than other times.

1. **Day In the Life Of (DILO):** Take a very close look at the day of your key consumers – your boss, your spouse, your family, co-workers, friends. Is there an early morning ritual that your boss always indulges in, like a cup of coffee before he / she heads for their desk? Perhaps a colleague enjoys a stroll in the park during lunch? Does your spouse look forward to a quiet breakfast with you after the kids leave for activities on Sunday? Maybe your children value the time they spend with you just before bed? This exercise can be extremely informative if you are trying to figure out when your key consumers are most likely to be receptive to the new YOU!

2. **Year In the Life Of (YILO):** Do a similar exercise for the year at a macro level. During the year, there are certain times when your consumers will be more open than others. For example, your boss will certainly appreciate the new YOU! more during the annual business planning cycle, as your spouse would appreciate you more during the summer

months when the children are home and cannonballing around the house.

3. **Life Itself:** There will be things happening in the lives of your consumers that give you windows of opportunity as well. The boss's daughter's going away to college? Your mother-in-law is having knee replacement surgery? A colleague is going through a painful divorce? These are all opportunities to bring the new Brand YOU! to the fore.

So, once you have figured out WHEN to communicate the new Brand YOU, here is HOW you communicate to maximum advantage.

CHAPTER 25

Elements of the "Marketing Mix" for Brand YOU! (media, packaging, price, promotion etc...)

The great Dr. Philip Kotler in his seminal works on the business of marketing created the 4 Ps that every marketer in the world is aware of. They stand for Packaging, Promotion, Place and Price. Since then, these Ps have multiplied and become more and more narrowly defined.

The crux of it though is simple. **There are certain levers that you get to pull, certain buttons you get to push, when you are trying to build any brand, and many of them are applicable to Building Brand YOU.**

To keep things simple, I'm going to try to list some of them for you, but this list is by no means exhaustive. If you can think of things to add here, please let me know and I will make sure they are incorporated in future editions (hopefully there will be more than one edition ☺).

1. **Packaging:** How do you dress? How do you look? Our parents used to tell us that we have to "look the part", that when we go for a job interview, it's important to be 'suited up', with

shoes shined and shirt crisply ironed. You know what? They were right. The sad truth is that first impressions are created in the first 5-6 seconds of meeting someone. After that, we are just trying to justify them to ourselves. In today's casual era, the art of dressing up for an interview seems to be vanishing. I've seen candidates show up for an interview wearing jeans. While that may be acceptable and even required in some industries (software design, creative anything etc.), for the majority of office-based roles it is simply unacceptable. Evaluate yourself critically. Look at everything – body art, piercings, hair (colour, shape, size etc.) and figure out if what you see is actually right for you. If the answer is YES I love my hair and NO I've never seen a Finance Manager for a Fortune 500 company with blue hair, then you need to either change your hair or change your job ambition. For the ultra liberal readers out there, who will say that how a person looks should have no bearing on their ability to do a job, I say – I agree, in an ideal world. But if you live in a world where a person with extensive body piercings is instantly judged by clients and colleagues alike, and that impacts his or her ability to perform effectively in their role, then I would suggest its time to grow up and move forward.

2. **Communication:** What's your story? How do you present yourself?

    a. **Let's start with your handshake.** Firm, dry and brief while still meaningful are useful criteria. An ex-boss of mine had a handshake like a wet fish – shaking hands with him used to leave me surreptitiously wiping my hand on the seat of my pants. Others prefer the kung fu death grip, the silky caress of a seductress and so on. Feel free to add your own descriptors here... Remember, the purpose of shaking hands is to establish trust (hence the empty hand without a weapon!).

    b. **How about eye contact?** Many people say that it's difficult to trust someone, or engage with them, if they can't look you in the eyes. Do you find it difficult to make eye contact with people? Worse of all, are you one of those unfortunate people who's eyes always seem to be in an inappropriate place – let's say 12 inches south of where they ought to be? I can't tell you how disturbing that can be, and if you are not sure about where your eyes are going (albeit inadvertently), ask a close friend for feedback.

    c. **What about body language?** Are you aware of the signals your body language is sending? Body language is a science, and one worthy of study. Once you realize what a simple hand gesture can mean, or the relevance the most seemingly irrelevant movements can take on, a great deal more nuance and texture will appear in front of you. If you understand that up to 90% of all communication is in fact non-verbal (things your body says and does, not the words that come out of your mouth), and then you actual learn to "speak" that language, its like a light being switched on an a hitherto darkened room. I kid you not. Invest some time in this – it will pay you back in spades.

d. **How are your language skills?** Excellent, you say? I doubt that. No offense, but unless you are the exception that proves the rule, the odds are that you are a terrible communicator, in the written (think e-mail) as well as verbal form (think phone conferences, speaking to groups of people etc.). If you are the author of one of the hundreds of mails I receive daily, you use way too many acronyms, you misspell common words and use them interchangeably and inappropriately, your grammar is absolutely atrocious, and you have no idea what a proper sentence looks like. Do I sound ANAL? I know I do. But you have to realize that most people who are scanning through a 100+ resumes are looking for reasons to whittle down the list – and any of the errors mentioned above will likely help you get off that list quite quickly.

"That's not fair!" I can see you protesting. "They haven't gotten to know me!" That's right – and why should they? In the 5-6 second battle for the heart and mind, you have lost. The good news is – it's just a battle, not the war. You need to fix your language skills – again, an investment that is worth making.

e. **What about presentation skills?** Are you comfortable presenting in front of a small group of co-workers? How about a large group? The more senior you get, the more you will need to demonstrate an expertise in this area. I once knew someone who became semi-paralyzed at the idea of addressing an audience. He was – and probably still is – the most functionally competent person I know. His people skills are outstanding. But this area of his life left him shaken and stirred. Are you like this? If you are, you need to get over this fear somehow. I would suggest joining a group like Toastmasters, that teaches public speaking and encourages the overcoming of this most primal of fears. **BABAGOI. Build A Bridge And Get Over it.**

3. **Promotion:** How's your networking? Do you make an effort to meet new people? A fair measure of your networking skills is how many contacts you have on LinkedIn (if you are a working professional) or on Facebook

(for everyone else). If you are a professional and are not on LinkedIn, for goodness' sake, get over whatever is holding you back, and create a profile on LinkedIn today. I don't work for the company nor do I have any sort of relationship to them not have I received any form of compensation for what I'm about to explain to you. But if you are hesitant to get on LinkedIn because you don't know what to do, here is some advice on how to start:

a. When you sign up for LinkedIn, **make sure you provide a summary statement that truly encapsulates who you are.** You can use a slightly expanded version of your Brand Capsule for this.

b. **Fill out your profile to the maximum level possible.** Add all your jobs, along with what you accomplished at those jobs, to your profile. Add projects, interests and anything else that can give a viewer a more holistic view of who YOU are and what your brand stands for. LinkedIn shows a little graphic that allows you to track your profile completeness and makes useful suggestions to improve the strength of your profile further.

c. Once your profile has been saved and is viewable, **start adding connections.** Once again, LinkedIn has a great algorithm that suggests People You Might Know. Start by reaching out to those people whom you actually know – perhaps they are current co-workers, or past co-workers. **Try not to send the standard message that LinkedIn provides by default.** Using that message simply says that you can't be bothered to build your connections in a meaningful way. Instead, try to tailor that message in a way that allows you to build sustainable relationships. BTW, as soon as your profile is complete, you will start receiving invitations from people who know you, or want to connect with you.

d. **Build your network with some sort of strategy in mind.** If you work in Sales & Marketing, connect with professionals in your field. Connect with HR managers. Connect with recruiters. Connect with C-suite members inside and outside your organization, industry and geography. Once you **start networking with purpose**, it will be difficult to stop even if you wanted to.

e. **A general rule of thumb is that if you have over 500 connections on LinkedIn, you are serious about networking.** Do keep in mind that there are people with thousands of connections, so get cracking. You may have some serious catching up to do.

f. Please remember that **you should proactively network when you don't NEED to.** If you are looking for a job and start networking aggressively, people expect it and see through your efforts. Half of your contacts will start avoiding you, and the other half will be sympathetic but not really motivated to help. A few – a very few – might forward your CV to HR or to a recruiter. Now, if you have been proactively and empathetically networking, perhaps offering to help people with things that they don't really expect, what do you think will happen when they know you might need a little help yourself? This is a very basic philosophy in life – **what goes around, comes around.** Do unto others as you would have done unto you. Karma. Call it what you will. I'm not saying that everyone you know will suddenly rush to your aid – but you will certainly get a different response when your connections find out that you are looking for a new role. **This is especially true if you have successfully put in to practice the principles described in this book, and have created a BRAND that people are drawn to (BRAND PULL).** Then you won't have to do as much running around as you would otherwise. It will still take effort – finding a job is still a full-time job – but you will certainly be in a better place if people know what your brand stands for, the benefits your brand offers, and what you have accomplished.

g. If you, like hundreds of millions of people around the world, are addicted to Facebook, please be aware of the following:

 i. **If you post inappropriate pictures or comments on Facebook, you have to know that HR managers and recruitment consultants will discover those pictures and comments.** Trust me. The Internet is full of stories about people who have lost jobs, and potential jobs, because of exactly this. Be aware. Act smart.

 ii. **Facebook is a PERSONAL networking tool.** It helps you stay in touch with family and friends, so remember that when you start posting work-related stuff on there.

4. **Public Relations:** What do people say about you? Here again, LinkedIn is a brilliant tool. It has several feedback mechanisms that are built right in to the basic structure of your profile.

 a. **Recommendations** are a great way to know how people are viewing you professionally. Generally speaking, a profile with 20 recommendations is seen as stronger than one with 2. However, the quality of the reco is just as important. The words used, the length of the reco, and especially whom the reco is from.

Some advice – if you want a reco from someone, don't just up and ask them for a reco unless you are dead certain they will right you a good one. Recommend them, and they will probably return the favour. If they don't, that should tell you something.

b. **Endorsements:** Set up a bunch of skills that people can endorse you for. You might think that you are known for demonstrating certain skills, but in reality people value your work in another area. Someone I recently worked with switched careers from computing to HR, but people kept endorsing her work in IT because of a general lack of awareness in her professional circle that she had changed streams.

c. **Updates:** When you post an update on LinkedIn, which you should try to do once a week, how many people like and or respond to the update? Remember, your update goes to your entire list of connections, and their first-degree connections as well, so it can potentially be seen by a million or more people... so make each update a great one.

5. **Place:** The channels through which your Brand is "sold" or "bought". To put it briefly, if you have tried everything you can to get ahead in your current role or company, and are simply unable to move ahead, then it may

be time to move on. **Change the game.** Find a new role within your existing company, or get out there and start networking for your next job. **Find one that makes your heart sing,** and that is in line with the brand that you are trying to build – and don't compromise unless you are starving and about to end up on the street. For those people who are heading in to the job market right now, please remember that your chances of getting hired go up exponentially if people know what your Brand stands for, and they can see how you would be a good fit for the organization that you are applying at. And if there is no fit, then there is nothing to worry about. Get out there and hustle. Network. Connect with people. Pound the pavement. Press the flesh. **Be insistent. Be awesome.**

6. **Price: How much you are valued – your paycheck – depends on what you are perceived to bring to the table.** The key word is PERCEIVED. Remember the Brand Equity Cause & Effect ladder that I introduced you to in the earlier chapters of this book? **Your main job as the CEO of Brand YOU! is to create the right perception for your brand.** Once the hiring manager sitting across the table from you is convinced that you and only you can add the maximum value to the role that you are discussing, he or she will start to sell you on the company and why you should join them. When things move to

the next level, and you receive an offer from them, take your time before you say yes. It's perfectly OK to go back for clarifications, and sometimes, it's even better to say NO if you feel that the offer is too low, or can be made stronger. **The power of this word – NO – cannot be under-estimated.** But play this card carefully if at all – it can turn around and bite you.

And so on. **Remember, every action you take is either a DEPOSIT into, or a WITHDRAWAL from, the Bank of your Brand Equity.**

Build your brand with purpose and understand that everything you do impacts that.

This means everything, and I mean everything.

CHAPTER 26

Summary of the Plan for Brand YOU! (A game changer – taking control of YOUR personal & professional destiny)

So that's it. You are now ready to put the rubber to the road, the pedal to the metal, the plan in to action. **So what have we learned?**

We've learned that in order to build our own brands, **we must know who our target audience is, and we must start with understanding their needs** (consumer insight).

When we have understood them well enough to know what they NEED from you, we can figure out how to fulfill those needs. We also understand that we cannot possibly fulfill everyone's needs – **so we need to make CHOICES.** This involves us saying NO sometimes, but that is not a hurdle necessarily. It frees us up to say YES to things that are really important.

The next step is to **craft a unique and powerful Brand Identity for Brand YOU.** A document that truly encapsulates who you are, your strengths, your areas of opportunity, the things you want to build on and leverage as you move forward. This is your Perception Plan – how you want to be seen and acknowledged.

But **that plan**, if not brought to life in a compelling way, is just a document, a thought. It **needs to come alive in YOU**. Bring it to life in a way that is unmistakably YOU...

When you start to bring it to life, remember that every action you take, EVERY LITTLE THING you do (or don't do!) is either building your brand equity, or hurting it.

Armed with this knowledge, and the confidence that you now possess tools that have been used by millions of BRAND MANAGERS all over the world to build brands, go out there and JUST DO IT.

That's all there is. If I can help you in any way, please let me know.

All the best, and God Speed.

Omar